THRIVE IN THE YEAR OF THE HORSE

Chinese Zodiac Horoscope 2026

Linda Dearsley

BENNION KEARNY

Published in 2025 by Bennion Kearny

ISBN: 978-1-915855-43-5

Linda Dearsley has asserted her right under the Copyright, Designs and Patents Act, 1988 to be identified as the author of this book.

Copyright 2024. All Rights Reserved. No part of this publication may be reproduced, stored in a retrieval system, or transmitted in any form or by any means, electronic, mechanical, photocopying, recording or otherwise, without the prior permission of the publisher.

Bennion Kearny does not have any control over, or any responsibility for, any author or third-party websites mentioned in or on this publication.

A CIP catalogue record for this book is available from the British Library.

This book is sold subject to the condition that it shall not, by way of trade or otherwise, be lent, re-sold, hired out or otherwise circulated without the publisher's prior consent in any form of binding or cover other than that in which it is published and without a similar condition including this condition being imposed on the subsequent purchaser.

TABLE OF CONTENTS

CHAPTER 1: SUCCESS IN THE YEAR OF THE HORSE 1

Welcome Horse 1
So, What Just Happened? 2
Hidden Depths 2
Racing to the Rescue 2
Freedom and Change 2
The Awesome Power of Fire 3
Tame the Horse 3
Becoming a Horse Whisperer 4
Shout at Them and They Get Scared… 4
It's All About the Zeitgeist, Baby 4
Horses for Courses 5
Meet the Fantastic Fire Horse of 1966 – Absolutely Fabulous in Every Way 6
Young, Free and Trendy 6
Working Class Heroes 6
Forget Politics – Everyone's Watching the Footie 7
Champions of the World 7
Action, Action, Everywhere 8
Raring to Go 8
To Boldly Go Where No Man Has Gone Before… 8
Culture Gallops Far Out 9
Cars Go Groovy 9
Bolting the Stable Door 10
The Clocks Stopped at 9.13 10
A Noise Like Thunder, then the Mountain Collapsed 10
Playing with Fire… 11
Five Centuries of Flames 11
1906… 11

…and Then There Was 1846… 11
…Plus 1726… 12
…and Not Forgetting the Memorable Fire Horse of 1666 12
Introducing… The Charismatic Crimson Horse of 2026 12
USA in the Spotlight 13
Fireworks to Die For 13
Happy Birthday, Mr President 13
and Then There's the Footie 14
No Such Thing as Too Much Sport 14
Climbing Off the Couch 14
Taking to the Streets 14
The Call of the Wild 14
Why Is The Year Called Horse? 15
How to Succeed in 2026 17
    Find Your Chinese Astrology Sign 18
    And there's More to it Than That 18
The Meaning of Your Chinese Numbers 22

CHAPTER 2: THE HORSE 24

Will 2026 be a Glorious Year for the Horse? 24
The Wonder of Being a Horse 26
The Horse Home 28
Being Friends with the Horse 28
Horse Superpowers 29
Best Jobs for Horse 2026 29
Perfect Partners 29
Horse Love 2026 Style 31
Secrets of Success in 2026 32
The Horse Year at a Glance 32

CHAPTER 3: THE GOAT 34

Will 2026 be a Glorious Year for the Goat? 34
The Wonder of Being a Goat 36
The Goat home 38
Being Friends with the Goat 38
Goat Superpowers 39
Best Jobs for Goat 2026 39
Perfect Partners 39
Goat Love 2026 Style 41
Secrets of Success in 2026 42
The Goat Year at a Glance 43

CHAPTER 4: THE MONKEY 45

Will 2026 be a Glorious Year for the Monkey? 45
The Wonder of Being a Monkey 47
The Monkey Home 48
Being Friends with the Monkey 48
Monkey Superpowers 49
Best Jobs 2026 49
Perfect Partners 49
Monkey Love 2026 Style 52
Secrets of Success in 2026 52
The Monkey Year at a Glance 53

CHAPTER 5: THE ROOSTER 55

Will 2026 be a Golden Year for the Rooster? 55
The Wonder of Being a Rooster 57
The Rooster Home 58
Being Friends with the Rooster 58
Rooster Superpowers 59
Best Jobs for Rooster 2026 59

 Perfect Partners 59
 Rooster Love 2026 Style 62
 Secrets of Success in 2026 62
 The Rooster Year at a Glance 63

CHAPTER 6: THE DOG 65
 Will 2026 be a Glorious Year for the Dog? 65
 The Wonder of Being a Dog 67
 The Dog Home 68
 Being Friends with the Dog 69
 Dog Superpowers 69
 Best Jobs for Dog 2026 69
 Perfect Partners 70
 Dog Love 2026 Style 72
 Secrets of Success in 2026 73
 The Dog Year at a Glance 73

CHAPTER 7: THE PIG 75
 Will 2026 be a Glorious Year for the Pig? 75
 The Wonder of Being a Pig 77
 The Pig Home 78
 Being Friends with the Pig 79
 Pig Superpowers 79
 Best Jobs for Pig 2026 79
 Perfect Partners 80
 Pig Love 2026 Style 82
 Secrets of Success in 2026 82
 The Pig Year at a Glance 83

CHAPTER 8: THE RAT 85
 Will 2026 be a Glorious Year for the Rat? 85

The Wonder of Being a Rat 87
The Rat Home 89
Being Friends with the Rat 89
Rat Superpowers 89
Best Jobs for Rat in 2026 89
Perfect Partners 2026 90
Rat Love 2026 Style 92
Secrets of Success in 2026 93
The Rat Year at a Glance 94

CHAPTER 9: THE OX 96
Will 2026 be a Glorious year for the Ox? 96
The Wonder of Being an Ox 98
The Ox Home 100
Being Friends with the Ox 100
Ox Superpowers 101
Best Jobs for Ox 2026 101
Perfect Partners 101
Ox Love 2026 Style 103
Secrets of Success in 2026 104
The Ox Year at a Glance 105

CHAPTER 10: THE TIGER 107
Will 2026 be a Glorious Year for the Tiger? 107
The Wonder of Being a Tiger 109
The Tiger Home 110
Being Friends with the Tiger 111
Tiger Superpowers 111
Best Jobs for Tiger 2026 111
Perfect Partners 112
Tiger Love 2026 Style 114

Secrets of Success in 2026 115
The Tiger Year at a Glance 115

CHAPTER 11: THE RABBIT 117
Will 2026 be a Glorious Year for the Rabbit? 117
The Wonder of Being a Rabbit 119
The Rabbit Home 120
Being Friends with the Rabbit 121
Rabbit Superpowers 121
Best Jobs for Rabbit 2026 121
Perfect Partners 121
Rabbit Love 2026 Style 124
Secrets of Success in 2026 124
The Rabbit Year at a Glance 125

CHAPTER 12: THE DRAGON 127
Will 2026 be a Glorious Year for the Dragon? 127
The Wonder of Being a Dragon 129
The Dragon Home 130
Being Friends with the Dragon 131
Dragon Superpowers 131
Best Jobs for Dragon 2026 131
Perfect Partners 132
Dragon Love 2026 Style 134
Secrets of Success in 2026 135
The Dragon Year at a Glance 135

CHAPTER 13: THE SNAKE 137
Will 2026 be a Glorious Year for the Snake? 137
The Wonder of Being a Snake 139
The Snake Home 141

Being Friends with the Snake 141

Snake Superpowers 141

Best Jobs for Snake 2026 142

Perfect Partners 142

Snake Love 2026 Style 144

Secrets of Success in 2026 145

The Snake Year at a Glance 145

CHAPTER 14: BUT THEN THERE'S SO MUCH MORE TO YOU 148

Your Outer Animal – (Birth Year | Creates Your First Impression) 148

Your Inner Animal – (Birth Month | The Private You) 149

    Month of Birth - Your Inner Animal 149

Your Secret Animal – (Birth Hour | The Still, Small Voice Within) 149

    Hours of Birth – Your Secret Animal 150

CHAPTER 15: IN YOUR ELEMENT 151

Metal 155

Water 155

Wood 156

Fire 156

Earth 157

Yin and Yang 158

Friendly Elements 160

Unfriendly Elements 160

CHAPTER 16: WESTERN HOROSCOPES AND CHINESE HOROSCOPES – THE LINK 161

Horse 162

    Aries Horse 162

Taurus Horse	162
Gemini Horse	162
Cancer Horse	162
Leo Horse	163
Virgo Horse	163
Libra Horse	163
Scorpio Horse	163
Sagittarius Horse	164
Capricorn Horse	164
Aquarius Horse	164
Pisces Horse	164
Goat	165
Aries Goat	165
Taurus Goat	165
Gemini Goat	165
Cancer Goat	165
Leo Goat	165
Virgo Goat	166
Libra Goat	166
Scorpio Goat	166
Sagittarius Goat	166
Capricorn Goat	167
Aquarius Goat	167
Pisces Goat	167
Monkey	167
Aries Monkey	167
Taurus Monkey	167
Gemini Monkey	168
Cancer Monkey	168
Leo Monkey	168
Virgo Monkey	168
Libra Monkey	169
Scorpio Monkey	169

- Sagittarius Monkey..........169
- Capricorn Monkey..........169
- Aquarius Monkey..........169
- Pisces Monkey..........170

Rooster..........170
- Aries Rooster..........170
- Taurus Rooster..........170
- Gemini Rooster..........170
- Cancer Rooster..........170
- Leo Rooster..........171
- Virgo Rooster..........171
- Libra Rooster..........171
- Scorpio Rooster..........171
- Sagittarius Rooster..........171
- Capricorn Rooster..........172
- Aquarius Rooster..........172
- Pisces Rooster..........172

Dog..........172
- Aries Dog..........172
- Taurus Dog..........172
- Gemini Dog..........173
- Cancer Dog..........173
- Leo Dog..........173
- Virgo Dog..........173
- Libra Dog..........173
- Scorpio Dog..........174
- Sagittarius Dog..........174
- Capricorn Dog..........174
- Aquarius Dog..........174
- Pisces Dog..........174

Pig..........175
- Aries Pig..........175
- Taurus Pig..........175

- Gemini Pig 175
- Cancer Pig 175
- Leo Pig 175
- Virgo Pig 176
- Libra Pig 176
- Scorpio Pig 176
- Sagittarius Pig 176
- Capricorn Pig 176
- Aquarius Pig 177
- Pisces Pig 177

Rat 177
- Aries Rat 177
- Taurus Rat 177
- Gemini Rat 178
- Cancer Rat 178
- Leo Rat 178
- Virgo Rat 178
- Libra Rat 179
- Scorpio Rat 179
- Sagittarius Rat 180
- Capricorn Rat 180
- Aquarius Rat 180
- Pisces Rat 180

Ox 181
- Aries Ox 181
- Taurus Ox 181
- Gemini Ox 181
- Cancer Ox 182
- Leo Ox 182
- Virgo Ox 182
- Libra Ox 183
- Scorpio Ox 183
- Sagittarius Ox 183

 Capricorn Ox 184
 Aquarius Ox 184
 Pisces Ox 184
Tiger 185
 Aries Tiger 185
 Taurus Tiger 185
 Gemini Tiger 185
 Cancer Tiger 185
 Leo Tiger 186
 Virgo Tiger 186
 Libra Tiger 186
 Scorpio Tiger 186
 Sagittarius Tiger 187
 Capricorn Tiger 187
 Aquarius Tiger 187
 Pisces Tiger 188
Rabbit 188
 Aries Rabbit 188
 Taurus Rabbit 188
 Gemini Rabbit 188
 Cancer Rabbit 189
 Leo Rabbit 189
 Virgo Rabbit 189
 Libra Rabbit 189
 Scorpio Rabbit 189
 Sagittarius Rabbit 190
 Capricorn Rabbit 190
 Aquarius Rabbit 190
 Pisces Rabbit 190
Dragon 191
 Aries Dragon 191
 Taurus Dragon 191
 Gemini Dragon 191

    Cancer Dragon 192
    Leo Dragon 192
    Virgo Dragon 192
    Libra Dragon 192
    Scorpio Dragon 192
    Sagittarius Dragon 193
    Capricorn Dragon 193
    Aquarius Dragon 193
    Pisces Dragon 194
Snake 194
    Aries Snake 194
    Taurus Snake 194
    Gemini Snake 194
    Cancer Snake 194
    Leo Snake 195
    Virgo Snake 195
    Libra Snake 195
    Scorpio Snake 196
    Sagittarius Snake 196
    Capricorn Snake 196
    Aquarius Snake 196
    Pisces Snake 197

CHAPTER 17: CREATE A WONDERFUL YEAR 198

CHAPTER 1: SUCCESS IN THE YEAR OF THE HORSE

Welcome Horse

Okay, so dig out your shades, surround yourself with non-flammable materials, check the smoke alarm, then stand well back… and get ready to welcome the Year of the Horse.

For this is not just any old horse. As dawn breaks on February 17th 2026, the world will vibrate to the sound of pounding hoofbeats as the spectacular, show-stopping Crimson Fire Horse leaps onto the scene in a blaze of flying sparks and flaming hooves.

And while the cosmic equine scorches a smoking path into the Chinese New Year, the old Wood Snake of 2025 can only slither rapidly away for fear of getting burned to a crisp.

Just as well, because the impatient Horse has no time for Snake's subtle, tricksy ways. And Horse intends to canter, star of the show and downright gorgeous, right through the months until February 5th 2027.

So, if you've grown tired of 2025's exhausting atmosphere of political intrigue, plots within plots, and ceaseless arguments about conspiracy theories, then the straightforward Horse energy of 2026 could come as a welcome relief.

But don't be fooled. The Year of the Crimson Horse might offer a refreshing contrast to last year's reign of the serpent, but not necessarily a relaxing contrast. The action-loving Horse can't stand still for long, but if you saddle up and hang on tight, it could be the exhilarating ride of your life.

So, What Just Happened?

If the year just passed struck you as an endless succession of claims and counterclaims – protests, back-stabbings, and general scheming behind the scenes – you're not alone. 2025 was a typical Snake year. Snakes might present as quiet, modest, unobtrusive types, but they can move with surprising speed and cover a lot of ground, while remaining completely hidden. And cerebral Snakes demand more intricate moves than a Rubik's Cube, so it's no wonder events start resembling the most convoluted spy drama when Snake energy is in charge. Plus, of course, Snakes can strike with swift, deadly venom when annoyed. So 2025 witnessed some sudden, unexpected, and not particularly pleasant shocks.

Hidden Depths

Yet despite (or maybe because of) all this, a lot of change is accomplished during a Snake year – we just don't tend to realise it until much later.

So, if you couldn't work out quite what was really going on back in 2025 but had the feeling something significant was afoot, you're probably right. And we might find out exactly what Snake was up to when Horse starts kicking up the dust of 2026.

Racing to the Rescue

Intrigue has its uses, of course, but enough is enough as far as straightforward Horse energy is concerned. Life's too short for the sort of complicated, double-edged, often insincere diplomacy at which the Snake excels. Passionate Horse regards such sophistry as a waste of time. Just 'get on with it' is the Horse's motto, and you might as well make your intentions crystal clear while you're at it.

It's no accident that a bracingly energetic Horse year always follows a multi-layered Snake reign in the Chinese tradition. Ancient, oriental wisdom asserts that all creation strives for balance, so after 12 long months of soaking up inscrutable, serpent energy, the world is desperate for a clean, clear antidote.

Which is exactly where the splendid Horse prances in.

Freedom and Change

In Chinese tradition, the horse is much admired and associated with freedom and vitality. Just as we delight in the sight of wild horses galloping joyfully across a seashore, manes flying, all cares forgotten – during a Horse year, a similar longing for wide open spaces and a throwing off of restrictions tends to sweep the world.

Horse years are renowned for bold action, a revival of independent spirit, and impatience with rules and regulations. So, if you loathe bureaucracy and the constraints of small print, this might just be the year you throw caution to the wind, tear up the whole lot, and rebel.

Wisdom of the Horse

Life is where you're at. Whatever you're doing, it's enough.

Cindy Crawford
(1966 Fire Horse)

The Awesome Power of Fire

The other thing that marks the atmosphere of 2026 as noticeably different from the past two years is that the governing element has changed. In Chinese tradition, each year (as well as being ruled by a zodiac animal) comes marinated in the qualities of a natural element.

In 2024 and 2025, that element was Wood which, according to oriental lore, represents growth and expansion. But in 2026, the Horse ushers in the first of two years crackling with the vibrant energy of the Fire element. And after 24 months of all that glorious Wood fuel building up ahead of the Horse's entrance, the Fire year of 2026 promises to be a blazing spectacular.

Fire years are believed to be lively, fast-paced, and exciting, but there is also the potential for conflict, so cool heads need to prevail.

Tame the Horse

So, what will the Year of the Horse bring to you? Will you have the cosmic equine eating out of your hand and transporting you majestically to your own personal winning post? Or will you accidentally spook it and send it galloping for the hills, taking all its golden potential with it and leaving you lost and stranded somewhere you've no wish to be?

For, annoyingly, despite the Horse's large, strong physique, it startles incredibly easily. The wrong move can cause it to bolt without warning, never to return.

Yet there's no need to worry. According to Chinese astrology, it's perfectly possible to tame the Horse with a little bit of thought and forward planning.

True, some signs are naturally more on the thoroughbred's wavelength than others, so they don't have to work as hard, but even those signs that can hardly distinguish a horse from a dairy cow can learn how to win the equine's trust.

Becoming a Horse Whisperer

The secret to befriending the Horse is deceptively simple. Once you understand the nature of the beast, how it gets on with your own particular sign and why, the way ahead becomes clear. As soon as you know what you're dealing with, you can formulate a plan. As Carl Sagan surmised: 'You have to know the past to understand the present.'

Shout at Them and They Get Scared…

Musician Paul McCartney, a born Water Horse (1942) and therefore particularly sensitive to all matters cosmic equine, instinctively understands what makes the Horse tick. Here, he's talking about how to sing into a microphone, but his advice holds just as good for handling the Horse.

'Microphones are like people (or Horses),' he said, 'Shout at them and they get scared.'

Once you know, no matter how bold or threatening events appear at first sight, if you take Paul's advice this year, you might find it far easier to defuse any situation with a very firm response than you ever imagined.

In turn, if you're trying to seal a deal or be chosen for promotion, just recall Paul's words, curb your impatience, and opt for a gentle, softly-softly approach. It could work wonders.

It's All About the Zeitgeist, Baby

Things were different last year, of course. Try such tactics on the wily Snake of 2025, and at best you'd end up with a glacial stare, at worst, a poisonous fang sunk deep in your leg.

That's why, as irritating as it may seem, it's worth finding out what you're up against in the coming 12 months. It's no good assuming what worked well for you last year will be just as successful in 2026. Clever types will alter their strategy to suit the new energy.

They just 'get' that the same eat-drink-and-be-merry attitude that will make you the toast of a Pig Year, is likely to land you unemployed and homeless when hard-working Ox is ruling the roost. Or that a cheeky, riotous prank that wins you your own TV show in a Monkey Year is likely to get you cancelled, when serious-minded Tiger is in charge.

Many people can't be bothered to change, of course. They do what they do – just as they always have done – and they're not prepared to rethink. They never question why some years go well for them and others fall flat.

Yet, canny souls who align their plans with the horsey zeitgeist are likely to streak to success.

Wisdom of the Horse

> I'm one extreme or the other. I'm not good at doing moderation.
>
> **Margot Robbie**
> (1990 Metal Horse)

Horses for Courses

The other thing to remember is that while all Horse years share the same basic 'horsiness', the zodiac Horse comes in five different varieties, breeds as it were – dressed in the colours of their particular year, each with their own distinct way of expressing their equine personality.

In the coming decades, we'll meet the Silver Metal Horse, the Brown Earth Horse, the Blue Water Horse, and (if we live long enough), the Green Wood Horse, because each element meets each equine only once every 60 years.

But right now, 2026 belongs to the Crimson Fire Horse, and we won't see its like again until 2086, so we need to make the most of it. Since the natural element of the Horse is also Fire, a fiery Horse ruling a Fire year is likely to be the wildest, most excitingly combustible of the lot.

So, it looks like we're in for a real red-letter year *in every way*. And to get an idea of how 2026 might shape up, we can check out what happened *the last time* the Crimson Fire Horse smouldered across the world stage – six whole decades ago, way back in 1966.

Meet the Fantastic Fire Horse of 1966 – Absolutely Fabulous in Every Way

The great thing about 1966 (if you happen to be British and more specifically English) was that 1966 was *your* year. For some reason, the passionate Fire Horse fell in love with England, and while the crush lasted, it showered the country with a glamour and good fortune that has rarely been equalled since.

Time Magazine dubbed London 'The Swinging City'; Beatlemania, the worldwide adoration of the UK's most famous rock band was at its height; and the astonishing, photographic model, Twiggy – a Londoner and the opposite of previous icons of female beauty with her flat chest, skinny legs and boyish hair-cut – was crowned Face of '66 and became an international star.

Thanks to the post-WWII baby boom, around 40 percent of the population was under 25, and youth culture, already well established, now exploded. Mini-skirts rose to eye-watering heights and many a young woman could no longer risk ascending the stairs of a double-decker bus. Union Jacks or stylised Mary Quant flowers decorated every possible item from mugs and cushions to household furniture, street signs, and clothes.

Suddenly, England was *the* place to be, and tourists from all over the world flocked in.

Young, Free and Trendy

Under the influence of the freedom-loving Horse, young people were incinerating the stuffy traditions and sober attitudes of the past. Safe, steady careers that their parents favoured were abandoned for newly cool professions. Everyone yearned to be a musician, or a model, a photographer, or a hairdresser. Achingly hip films such as Blow Up (about a photographer), Alfie (about a promiscuous chauffeur), and Darling (about a model in Swinging London, for which British actress Julie Christie won an Oscar that year) captured the mood.

Working Class Heroes

Once, people strived to emulate the aristocracy; now it was hip to be a working class hero. The Queen's sister, Princess Margaret, anticipated the trend by marrying commoner Anthony Armstrong-Jones back in 1960, and by '66 was roaring around town on the back of her husband's motorbike, blasting down country lanes in a souped-up Mini, and socialising with pop stars.

Genuine debs and titled youths adopted fake Liverpudlian or Cockney accents and kept quiet about the stately home and the inheritance.

Egalitarian pop culture was 'in'; everything else was out, and nobody wanted to be 'square'.

'It's often explained as a result of the post-World War II kids all coming of age at just the right time,' recalled Paul McCartney, 'And we all ended up in the same city. The Beatles had come down from Liverpool, other people had come over from America, the global village was just beginning and opening its doors. We went to the same parties, same galleries. It was a scene... The swinging London scene.'

Forget Politics – Everyone's Watching the Footie

In Britain, Prime Minister Harold Wilson won a second election, giving the Labour Party a bigger majority. In China, the Cultural Revolution – forged by terrifying revolutionaries in blood red scarves – was in full swing, creating devastating destruction. And in the USA, President Lyndon Johnson was spending more and more time holed up in the White House to avoid the angry student sit-ins and fierce critics of the Vietnam War that confronted him wherever he went.

Yet, in the UK, politics passed most people by. The whole country was more interested in the football. Sport had taken a thrilling turn.

England happened to be hosting the World Cup that year, and for just over two glorious weeks in July 1966, football stars dominated the headlines. Amazingly, the England team not only got into the final, they actually won – beating West Germany 4-2.

Wisdom of the Horse

> I'm gonna do something really outrageous. I'm gonna tell the truth.
>
> **John Travolta**
> (1954 Wood Horse)

Champions of the World

At the end of the match, team captain Bobby Moore was presented with the golden Jules Rimet trophy by the Queen, cheered on by 32 million ecstatic UK TV viewers watching England's triumph, broadcast in black and white, from home. Around the world, another 400 million tuned in to catch the action.

Afterwards, the England heroes were feted at a banquet in a top London hotel attended by the Prime Minister, while outside, the whole city erupted in joy. Traffic came to a standstill, euphoric crowds danced in the streets, and merry supporters leapt into the fountains at Trafalgar Square.

'It's like VE night, election night and New Year's Eve all rolled into one,' said an AA patrolman on duty at the time. Later, the Royal Mail issued a special 4d stamp marked 'England Winners' to commemorate the success. The players were awarded medals, and the whole country basked in reflected glory for months.

The victory has never been repeated since.

Action, Action, Everywhere
Across the Atlantic, in New York, construction began on what was to become the iconic World Trade Centre, destined to be the tallest building in the world for a while. In England, meanwhile, a more modest but strikingly original project began. Longleat, the first drive-through safari park outside Africa, opened its doors. Astonished visitors were invited to steer their cars nervously through bands of prowling lions roaming free in the leafy meadows and steady drizzle of the Wiltshire countryside!

Raring to Go
The Fire Horse never could resist a race, of course, especially if it involves flaming rocket boosters and heart-stopping speeds, so when Russia succeeded in soft landing a spacecraft – Luna 9 – on the moon in early February 1966 at the very end of the Snake year; it triggered what seemed to be an instant acceleration of the US/Soviet Union space race. Within weeks, in March, the US retaliated by dispatching astronauts Neil Armstrong and David Scott, aboard Gemini 8, to perform the first successful docking of two craft in space.

In response, in April, Russia launched Luna 10, which became the first spacecraft to orbit the Moon.

So, in May, the US launched Surveyor 1, which landed on the Moon, and followed it up with Lunar Orbiter 1, which took the first photograph of Earth from the Moon's orbit.

For the bemused public, it was like spectating a cosmic tennis match.

To Boldly Go Where No Man Has Gone Before…
Few could become real-life astronauts or experience the thrill of space, of course, but wannabees were able to get a taste from the latest US TV show. The international cult series Star Trek made its debut in

1966. While not an instant success, the show inspired tremendous devotion from fans. It wasn't long before the phenomenon of Trekkies and Star Trek conventions was born – and it's been going strong ever since.

Over in the UK, TV time and space traveller Dr Who continued to fascinate, so much so that a spin-off film, Daleks Invasion of the Earth (set in 2150 London), was rushed onto movie screens. And discreetly, away from the public gaze, another space sensation was being quietly constructed at Elstree Studios. Director Stanley Kubrick was overseeing the creation of Discovery One, the futuristic spaceship and star of his iconic movie masterpiece: 2001: A Space Odyssey.

Culture Gallops Far Out

Throughout 1966, the Beatles were still dominating the music scene, but artistic inspiration was changing. A new word was creeping into the national vocabulary – 'psychedelic'. This described a style of music, art, and fashion influenced by drugs, in particular, the latest must-have: LSD.

Credited with heightening creativity and expanding the mind, artists everywhere were experimenting with the new miracle. Soon, a hallucinatory quality began seeping into the Western world. Wild, swirling patterns and vibrant, clashing colours started to appear everywhere. Clothes, cars, and the sides of buildings exploded with crazed designs. Anything that could be decorated received a psychedelic makeover.

Cars Go Groovy

George Harrison had his trendy Mini Cooper (previously a smart, metallic black) repainted fiery red and smothered in gaudy, multi-coloured symbols. Then, he went on to have the interior of his home done up in a similar style. John Lennon admired George's Mini so much that when his Rolls-Royce – the ultimate luxury status-symbol, favoured by Royals and millionaires alike and usually seen only in elegantly understated black – was damaged while filming in Spain, he commissioned an artist to give it a psychedelic revamp. Traditionalists were shocked when it reappeared the following year, unrecognisable in dazzling yellow-gold, swathed with floral scrolls and flourishes. It seems the prestige car company was not too impressed. 'I am afraid the car is Mr. *Lennon's* property,' commented a Rolls-Royce spokesman sniffily at the time, 'and he is at liberty to do with it as he pleases.'

Bolting the Stable Door

By the middle of the year, the LSD revolution had mushroomed so fast that the drug was banned in the USA, and the following year Britain followed suit. But it was too late. The In Crowd was hooked, and 'acid' use carried on, underground.

But, imperceptibly, the attention of the Fire Horse was moving elsewhere. Over in California, a city the Crimson equine already knew well – San Francisco – began to capture the Horse's attention. That year, young people brought together over their shared love of drugs and loathing of the Vietnam War, began gravitating spontaneously to the Haight-Ashbury district of the city, forming 'hip' pacifist communities and calling themselves 'Hippies'. Soon, a distinctive West Coast sound was born, epitomised by bands such as the Beach Boys and the Mamas and Papas. The big 1966 hit, 'California Dreamin' by the Mamas and Papas, captured the mood perfectly.

Wisdom of the Horse

A good man always knows his limitations.

Clint Eastwood
(1930 Metal Horse)

The Clocks Stopped at 9.13

Bold, colourful and exciting the Fire Horse may be, but it also has its dark side. In 1966, the UK enjoyed so much good fortune that it was perhaps inevitable the luck would eventually run out, and it did, towards the end of the year, just as a rainy autumn set in.

A little after 9 am on the morning of October 21st 1966, the coal mining village of Aberfan at the foot of the Merthyr Mountain in Wales was just starting its day. At Pantglas School on the edge of the village, the children were excitedly opening their books on the last day before their half-term holiday.

A Noise Like Thunder, then the Mountain Collapsed

A few minutes later, a strange, rumbling roar, like thunder, or a vast jet taking off, froze them in their seats. The next second, tons and tons of colliery waste that had been piled for years in a huge heap on the mountainside above, suddenly collapsed and slid towards the village, racing downhill at speeds reaching 80 miles an hour. In moments, the black landslide engulfed the school, burying it under 40ft of debris. The hands on the school clock, unearthed later, were stopped forever at 9.13.

One hundred and sixteen children and 28 adults died that day. One of the teachers, David Beynon, was found in the wreckage cradling five of his pupils in his arms. They were all dead.

When the famously stoic Queen Elizabeth visited the scene a few days afterwards, she wept.

Playing with Fire...
In a word – don't. Just don't!

While it's true Fire Horse years can be exciting and exhilarating, there's no avoiding the fact that if you play with fire, you're likely to get burned. Fire is dangerous as well as beautiful. And when ushered in on the back of wild, Horse energy, the tiniest spark can rage out of control all too easily.

We tend to forget this, as there are usually only one or two Fire Horse years per century, so many people will not have encountered this energy before. But just look at what happened during some of the Fire Horse years of the distant past.

Five Centuries of Flames

1906...
Who recalls now that the Fire Horse year preceding 1966 was 1906, famous for the devastating San Francisco earthquake? While the quake, estimated to have been 7.9 on the later Richter scale, was destructive, it was actually fire that did the most damage. The quake ruptured gas lines, power lines, and gas lamps across the city, sparking countless small fires that quickly merged into an inferno. Firefighters struggled in vain to douse the flames because the water mains were broken, as well. By the time the blaze subsided, several days later, 80% of the city was gone.

...and Then There Was 1846...
The Fire Horse that preceded 1906 galloped through in 1846, leaving scorching hoof-prints in Canada and also the USA. In St John's, Newfoundland, Canada, a glue pot boiled over in a cabinetmaker's shop, igniting a fire that destroyed 2,000 buildings and left 12,000 people homeless. The same year in Nantucket, Massachusetts, a small

blaze in a hat shop leapt rapidly through wooden buildings that also stored whale oil, causing a conflagration that wiped out one-third of the town.

…Plus 1726…

The Fire Horse of 1786 turned out to be a relatively quiet, tame beast, but possibly only because grandpa Fire Horse of 1726 had staged such a spectacular. That year, a Portuguese galleon, the Santa Rosa, pride of the Portuguese fleet, laden with gold, diamonds, tobacco, sugar, and up to 200 barrels of gunpowder, suddenly exploded dramatically in the waters off Brazil, igniting a firework display to outdo all firework displays, killing 700 people on board. Only seven sailors survived the tragedy.

…and Not Forgetting the Memorable Fire Horse of 1666

…which cantered into England that year, inspiring the Great Fire of London, which began in a baker's shop in Pudding Lane. Around 80 per cent of the country's capital was destroyed by the flames, including 13,200 houses, 87 churches, and the city's great cathedral of St Paul's. It is thought that 70,000-80,000 people were left homeless.

It is very likely the Fire Horse's pyromaniac tendencies can be traced back even further, right into the mists of time, but let's not go there! Just keep the matches hidden away and take care.

Wisdom of the Horse

Becoming yourself is really hard and confusing.

Emma Watson
(1990 Metal Horse)

Introducing… The Charismatic Crimson Horse of 2026

So, after a brief round-up of the Fire Horse's exploits last time the world was treated to the Equine way, how will the brand new Horse adapt to our modern era? What can we expect from 2026?

For a start, as the Wood Snake slithers away, exhausted from all that intrigue, we may notice a welcome brightening of the atmosphere. Red is the luckiest colour of them all, according to Chinese wisdom, so the dawning of a crimson year is an auspicious sign. Red attracts good fortune and vitality, so we could see more smiling faces everywhere we go. Suddenly, people will have a real spring in their step. Optimism will return.

The Snake constitution tires easily, which meant that last year, many sensed a general air of malaise hovering in the background. This should quickly evaporate in 2026 under the Horse's smouldering gaze. Horse is stamina on legs, and is born to run, so we can look forward to a huge surge of energy invigorating everything.

USA in the Spotlight

If 1966 could be said to have belonged to England, it looks as if 2026 will be the USA's chance to shine, and events in America this year will bring the Horse's inner show pony delightedly to the fore.

2026 marks the 250th anniversary of the signing of the US Declaration of Independence, and America is planning to party all year. The big day is July 4th, but President Trump is promising a whole 12 months of celebrations and shameless razzamatazz.

'They'll be held at every one of our National Parks, battlefields, and historic sites,' he announced.

Fireworks to Die For

Celebrities, sports stars, VIPs, and historians are expected to take part in the fun, and the centrepiece will be a 24-hour Disney production – Disney Celebrates America – which will highlight events from across the country and culminate (fittingly for the Fire Horse) in fireworks spectaculars from both Disney World and Disneyland. This extravaganza is expected to be so magnificent, it will make the rest of the World's usual New Year offerings look like a wet bonfire night in Slough.

Happy Birthday, Mr President

What's more, 2026 marks Donald Trump's 80th birthday, and he sees no reason to be coy or reticent about it. On the big day – June 14th – he intends to welcome the World to the White House, where he's hosting an Ultimate Fighting Championship event in the grounds.

'We have a lot of land there,' he explained. 'It's the ideal place.'

The Championship is planned to take place on the White House's extensive South Lawn, where the presidential helicopter usually lands.

A temporary arena with seating for approximately 5,000 spectators will be constructed, and the plan includes a large arch with a lighting grid to illuminate the scene. The White House will form the backdrop from one angle and the Washington Monument from another.

Bands will perform throughout the day, and screens will be set up so fans can watch the fights from other areas of the grounds.

Whatever happens, it will make headlines around the planet.

and Then There's the Footie

Just like England in 1966, the USA will be hosting the 2026 World Cup. To be fair, there are a few fixtures scheduled for Canada and Mexico, too, but the USA has the biggest share. From Los Angeles to Miami, from Boston to San Francisco, matches will be played across the entire country, and the whole jamboree culminates with the Cup Final in New York's New Jersey Stadium on July 19th.

No Such Thing as Too Much Sport

The athletic Horse very much encourages sport, and now and again in 2026, when the USA briefly relinquishes the spotlight, other countries take a turn in the arena. Italy hosts the Winter Olympics and Paralympics, Scotland gets the Commonwealth Games, and Australia and Papua New Guinea hold the 2026 Rugby League World Cup.

Climbing Off the Couch

But it's not just the professionals who'll enjoy the action. Restless Horse energy will sweep the land, inspiring even the most dedicated couch potato to get up, get fit, and maybe even join a gym. Public marathons will become more popular than ever, and there could be a resurgence of interest in horse racing and learning to ride.

Taking to the Streets

Back in '66, it was all about sit-ins but in '26, the Horse's instinct to herd together with like-minded friends and rebel will find expression in frequent, and frequently dramatic, protest marches and demonstrations. Things could get fiery – literally – if authority tries to clamp down. Expect wild clashes, thrown fireworks, and cars and buildings set ablaze if passions get out of hand. A herd of angry Horses quickly turns into a stampede as the police could find to their cost.

The Call of the Wild

At heart, of course, the Horse is a wild animal, and so we can expect a renewed longing for natural, open spaces, and unspoiled landscapes in

2026. Concern for the environment will become even more prominent, with opposition growing to net-zero policies that negatively affect rural views. At the same time, camping holidays, trekking expeditions, and country breaks will seem enticing, as well as festivals of every kind in the great outdoors, because the Horse loves to hang out with the herd.

Three Takeaways

A year that rewards openness
and no-nonsense behaviour

Heated words, anger, and bust-ups
will more easily surface

A year that rewards action. 'All talk and
no action types' will struggle

Why Is The Year Called Horse?
According to Chinese folklore, there are many explanations as to why the calendar is divided up the way it is. Perhaps the most popular is the story about the supreme Jade Emperor who lives in heaven. He decided to name each year in honour of a different animal and decreed that a race would be run to decide which animals would be chosen, and the order in which they would appear.

Twelve animals arrived to take part. Actually, in one legend, there were 13, including the Cat, who was a great friend of the Rat at the time. But the Cat was a sleepy creature and asked the Rat to wake him in time for the race. In the excitement (or was it by design?), the Rat forgot and dashed off, leaving the Cat fast asleep. The Cat missed the race and missed out on getting a year dedicated to his name. Which is why cats have hated rats ever since.

The Wily Rat and the Patient Ox

Anyway, as they approached the finish line, the 12 competitors found a wide river blocking their route. The powerful Ox, a strong swimmer, plunged straight in, but the tiny Rat begged to be carried across on his back. Kindly Ox agreed, but when they reached the opposite bank, the wily Rat scampered down Ox's body, jumped off his head and shot across the finish line in first place. Which is why the Rat is the first animal of the Chinese zodiac, followed by the Ox.

The Magnificent Tiger and the Ingenious Rabbit

The muscular Tiger, weighed down by his magnificent coat, arrived in third place, followed by the non-swimming Rabbit, who'd found some rocks downstream and hopped neatly from one to another until it spotted a log floating along and jumped on to be carried safely to dry land.

The Dragon Delayed

The Emperor was surprised to see the Dragon with his great wings, fly in, in fifth place, instead of the expected first. The Dragon explained that while high up in the sky, he saw a village in flames and the people running out of their houses in great distress, so he'd made a detour and employed his rain-making skills (Chinese Dragons can create water as well as fire) to put out the blaze before returning to the race. In some versions of the story, Dragon also adds that as he approached the river, he spotted poor little Rabbit clinging perilously to a log, so Dragon gently blew the log across and watched to see Rabbit safely ashore before flying over himself.

The Shrewd Snake and the Obliging Horse

In sixth place came the Snake. Clever as the Rat, the Snake had wrapped himself around one of the Horse's hooves and hung on while the Horse swam the river. When the Horse climbed ashore, the Snake slithered off, so startling the Horse that it reared up in alarm, allowing the Snake to slide over the finish line ahead of him.

The Three Musketeers: the Goat, the Monkey and the Rooster

The Goat, Monkey, and Rooster arrived next at the river. They spotted some driftwood and rope washed up on the shore, so Monkey deftly lashed them together to make a raft and the three of them hopped aboard and floated across. The Goat jumped off first, swiftly followed by Monkey and Rooster.

The Dallying Dog and the Hungry Pig

They found they'd beaten the Dog, which was unexpected as the Dog was a good swimmer. It turned out the Dog so enjoyed the water, he'd hung around playing in the shallows, emerging only in time to come eleventh. Last of all came the Pig, not the best of swimmers, and further slowed by his decision to pause for a good meal before exerting himself in the current.

The Wheel of the Zodiac is Complete

And so, the wheel of the zodiac was set forevermore, with the Year of the Rat beginning the cycle, followed by the Ox, Tiger, Rabbit, Dragon, Snake, Horse, Goat, Monkey, Rooster, Dog, and Pig.

How to Succeed in 2026

So, since 2026 is the Year of the Horse, how will you fare? Does the Horse present your astrological animal with opportunities or challenges? As the fable about how the years got their names shows, every one of the astrological animals is resourceful in its own special way. Faced with the prospect of crossing the river, each successfully made it to the other side, even the creatures that could barely swim.

So, whether your year animal gets on easily with the Crimson Fire Horse or whether they have to work at their relationship, you can make 2026 a special year to remember.

Chinese Astrology has been likened to a weather forecast. Once you know whether you'll need your umbrella or your suntan lotion, you can step out with confidence and enjoy the trip.

Find Your Chinese Astrology Sign

To find your Chinese sign, just look up your birth year in the table below.

Important note: if you were born in January or February, check the dates of the New Year very carefully. The Chinese New Year follows the lunar calendar and the beginning and end dates are not fixed, but vary each year. If you were born before mid-February, your animal sign might actually be the sign of the previous year. For example, 1980 was the year of the Monkey, but the Chinese New Year began on February 16, so a person born in January or early February 1980 would belong to the year before – the year of the Goat.

And there's More to it Than That...

In case you're saying to yourself, but surely, how can every person born in the same 365 days have the same personality(?) – you're quite right. The birth year is only the beginning.

Your birth year reflects the way others see you and your basic characteristics, but your month and time of birth are also ruled by the celestial animals – probably different animals from the one that dominates your birth year. The personalities of these other animals modify and add talents to those you acquired with your birth year creature.

The 1920s

5 February 1924 – 24 January 1925 | RAT

25 January 1925 – 12 February 1926 | OX

13 February 1926 – 1 February 1927 | TIGER

2 February 1927 – 22 January 1928 | RABBIT

23 January 1928 – 9 February 1929 | DRAGON

10 February 1929 – 29 January 1930 | SNAKE

The 1930s

30 January 1930 – 16 February 1931 | HORSE
17 February 1931 – 5 February 1932 | GOAT
6 February 1932 – 25 January 1933 | MONKEY
26 January 1933 – 13 February 1934 | ROOST5R
14 February 1934 – 3 February 1935 | DOG
4 February 1935 – 23 January 1936 | PIG
24 January 1936 – 10 February 1937 | RAT
11 February 1937 – 30 January 1938 | OX
31 January 1938 – 18 February 1939 | TIGER
19 February 1939 – 7 February 1940 | RABBIT

The 1940s

8 February 1940 – 26 January 1941 | DRAGON
27 January 1941 – 14 February 1942 | SNAKE
15 February 1942 – 4 February 1943 | HORSE
5 February 1943 – 24 January 1944 | GOAT
25 January 1944 – 12 February 1945 | MONKEY
13 February 1945 – 1 February 1946 | ROOSTER
2 February 1946 – 21 January 1947 | DOG
22 January 1947 – 9 February 1948 | PIG
10 February 1948 – 28 January 1949 | RAT
29 January 1949 – 16 February 1950 | OX

The 1950s

17 February 1950 – 5 February 1951 | TIGER
6 February 1951 – 26 January 1952 | RABBIT
27 January 1952 – 13 February 1953 | DRAGON
14 February 1953 – 2 February 1954 | SNAKE
3 February 1954 – 23 January 1955 | HORSE
24 January 1955 – 11 February 1956 | GOAT
12 February 1956 – 30 January 1957 | MONKEY
31 January 1957 – 17 February 1958 | ROOSTER
18 February 1958 – 7 February 1959 | DOG
8 February 1959 – 27 January 1960 | PIG

The 1960s

28 January 1960 – 14 February 1961 | RAT
15 February 1961 – 4 February 1962 | OX
5 February 1962 – 24 January 1963 | TIGER
25 January 1963 – 12 February 1964 | RABBIT
13 February 1964 – 1 February 1965 | DRAGON
2 February 1965 – 20 January 1966 | SNAKE
21 January 1966 – 8 February 1967 | HORSE
9 February 1967 – 29 January 1968 | GOAT
30 January 1968 – 16 February 1969 | MONKEY
17 February 1969 – 5 February 1970 | ROOSTER

The 1970s

6 February 1970 – 26 January 1971 | DOG
27 January 1971 – 14 February 1972 | PIG
15 February 1972 – 2 February 1973 | RAT
3 February 1973 – 22 January 1974 | OX
23 January 1974 – 10 February 1975 | TIGER
11 February 1975 – 30 January 1976 | RABBIT
31 January 1976 – 17 February 1977 | DRAGON
18 February 1977 – 6 February 1978 | SNAKE
7 February 1978 – 27 January 1979 | HORSE
28 January 1979 – 15 February 1980 | GOAT

The 1980s

16 February 1980 – 4 February 1981 | MONKEY
5 February 1981 – 24 January 1982 | ROOSTER
25 January 1982 – 12 February 1983 | DOG
13 February 1983 – 1 February 1984 | PIG
2 February 1984 – 19 February 1985 | RAT
20 February 1985 – 8 February 1986 | OX
9 February 1986 – 28 January 1987 | TIGER
29 January 1987 – 16 February 1988 | RABBIT
17 February 1988 – 5 February 1989 | DRAGON
6 February 1989 – 26 January 1990 | SNAKE

The 1990s

27 January 1990 – 14 February 1991 | HORSE
15 February 1991 – 3 February 1992 | GOAT
4 February 1992 – 22 January 1993 | MONKEY
23 January 1993 – 9 February 1994 | ROOSTER
10 February 1994 – 30 January 1995 | DOG
31 January 1995 – 18 February 1996 | PIG
19 February 1996 – 7 February 1997 | RAT
8 February 1997 – 27 January 1998 | OX
28 January 1998 – 5 February 1999 | TIGER
6 February 1999 – 4 February 2000 | RABBIT

The 2000s

5 February 2000 – 23 January 2001 | DRAGON
24 January 2001 – 11 February 2002 | SNAKE
12 February 2002 – 31 January 2003 | HORSE
1 February 2003 – 21 January 2004 | GOAT
22 January 2004 – 8 February 2005 | MONKEY
9 February 2005 – 28 January 2006 | ROOSTER
29 January 2006 – 17 February 2007 | DOG
18 February 2007 – 6 February 2008 | PIG
7 February 2008 – 25 January 2009 | RAT
26 January 2009 – 13 February 2010 | OX

The 2010s

14 February 2010 – 2 February 2011 | TIGER
3 February 2011 – 22 January 2012 | RABBIT
23 January 2012 – 9 February 2013 | DRAGON
10 February 2013 – 30 January 2014 | SNAKE
31 January 2014 – 18 February 2015 | HORSE
19 February 2015 – 7 February 2016 | GOAT
8 February 2016 – 27 January 2017 | MONKEY
28 January 2017 – 15 February 2018 | ROOSTER
16 February 2018 – 4 February 2019 | DOG
5 February 2019 – 24 January 2020 | PIG

The 2020s and a smidge beyond

25 January 2020 – 11 February 2021 | RAT
12 February 2021 – 31 January 2022 | OX
1 February 2022 – 21 January 2023 | TIGER
22 January 2023 – 9 February 2024 | RABBIT
10 February 2024 – 28 January 2025 | DRAGON
29 January 2025 – 16 February 2026 | SNAKE
17 February 2026 – 5 February 2027 | HORSE
6 February 2027 – 25 January 2028 | GOAT
26 January 2028 – 12 February 2029 | MONKEY
13 February 2029 – 2 February 2030 | ROOSTER
3 February 2030 - 22 January 2031 DOG
23 January 2031 – 10 February 2032 PIG

The Meaning of Your Chinese Numbers

Across the following zodiac chapters, each animal signs off with its lucky numbers for 2026. But what do the numbers represent? In turn, what happens when the lucky number for your sign happens to be an inauspicious (or unlucky) number? This seems a contradiction, but 'context is king'. For example, 5 is typically considered positive due to its association with the five elements (lucky), but the word sounds similar to 'not/without' in Chinese (i.e., unlucky). Also, a combination of numbers can make something perceived to be unlucky become lucky. Using our 5 example once again, when used in conjunction with 4 (i.e., 54), we create a 'without death' combination, which is surely good in the right context!

1: Number one symbolises independence and new beginnings. Yet it can be lonely.

2: Two is a lucky number representing harmony and companionship. It's believed that good things come in pairs.

3: Three is associated with growth, abundance, and stability.

4: The unluckiest number of them all, as four sounds like the word for death. Car number plates containing a four are avoided. Some buildings leave out the fourth floor altogether – as often happens with the number thirteen in the west. Ironically, thirteen is unloved in China too, as the digits add up to the unfortunate four.

5: Five is associated with the five Chinese elements – Water, Wood, Fire, Earth, Metal - which together provide perfect balance.

6: Six is auspicious since it sounds like the word for smooth flowing. Six in your orbit suggests plans will go well for you and obstacles will disappear.

7: Seven arouses mixed feelings. It can symbolise energy and growth, but also deception. An air of mystery surrounds a seven.

8: Eight is considered the luckiest number you can have as it's associated with wealth and prosperity. Number plates with the number 8 repeated, the eighth floor of any building, or a house number are highly sought after.

9: The last single digit number, nine, is the symbol of long life as it's the top of the list.

CHAPTER 2: THE HORSE

Horse Years

30 January 1930 – 16 February 1931

15 February 1942 – 4 February 1943

3 February 1954 – 23 January 1955

21 January 1966 – 8 February 1967

7 February 1978 – 27 January 1979

27 January 1990 – 14 February 1991

12 February 2002 – 31 January 2003

31 January 2014 – 18 February 2015

17 February 2026 – 5 February 2027

4 February 2038 – 23 January 2039

1 February 2041 – 21 January 2042

23 January 2050 – 10 February 2051

Natural Element: Fire

Will 2026 be a Glorious Year for the Horse?

Wow, Horse, you always suspected you were a bit of a superstar, but maybe no one else seemed to notice. Well, they will now! 2026 is *your* year. Step forward and do one of those theatrical circus bows. You could even add a feather plume if you really want to go for it. You might as well get in touch with your inner show pony because you're about to dazzle the world.

Sparkling Horse energy rules the planet for the next twelve months. Your values, your way of doing things, your unique perspective, and your sheer magnetism will influence everyone and everything until February 2027. Talk about power! Quite an ego blast, huh? You've waited a long time to be the boss – 12 whole years in fact, so it might take a week or two to get used to it.

You've had over a decade to plan for 2026 and how you were going to use your new role, of course, but if you're typical of your sign, you probably haven't given it much thought. You're always too busy dealing with the here and now to worry too much about the future.

Plus, of course, last year you had the Snake to contend with. It's not that the Snake has anything personal against you, Horse, it's just that the slippery serpent makes you nervous.

This possibly stems from some deep instinct formed after your namesake's unfortunate incident with the Jade Emperor and the River Race – when the unscrupulous Snake hitched a ride, uninvited, across the water wrapped around your leg, and cheated you out of what should have been sixth place ashore in the process. As a result, you're seventh on the cosmic calendar – destined to follow the Snake through the years for all eternity. No wonder you're not a big fan.

As such, 2025 might have been a bit of a struggle for a lot of Horses. Looking back, hopefully nothing drastic went wrong, but there were quite a few unexpected events – a Snake speciality – and you were forced to deal with them when you would have preferred not to. Nevertheless, admit it Horse, you enjoyed quite a few good times too. Even so, throughout the year, you probably felt a little lacklustre, a little more withdrawn than usual, without knowing why.

Well, you can forget about that now; Horse vitality is flooding back. Your confidence is exploding, and you can't wait to get started. Suddenly, you can think of a hundred projects you're itching to begin, and everywhere you look, people are falling over themselves to help you, such is your popularity right now.

This year, in fact, you're going to be more *authentically you*, more in sync with yourself, than you've possibly ever been, unless you were around in 1966. The reason is that the Horse is a Fire sign and 2026 is a Fire year. For the first time in 60 years, everything inside can now click into place for you. Many Horses will find that various internal struggles and insecurities just fade away as if they never existed.

The fiery atmosphere will boost your energy and inspire you to greater heights. Quite a few Horses changed jobs last year, influenced by the Snake's drive for change and transformation, yet now some equines might be regretting their decision. Not because they can't cope with the role, but because they didn't aim high enough.

No need to worry, Horse. Your exceptional talents are plain to see in 2026, and you can apply for something better or go for promotion, with success virtually guaranteed.

In the same way, many Horses found themselves new premises last year. But what seemed perfect back then could now begin to develop hidden faults. Either the property, the location, or the neighbours could turn out to be not quite as good as you expected. So quite a few equines could find themselves house hunting once again in 2026 or engaged in exciting renovations.

You've always been quietly ambitious if you're typical of your sign, Horse, and now, in your special year, you're fired up anew with a drive to improve every facet of your life. You've got the courage and the self-assurance to do it, too. And given your natural affinity with sport and the theatre, many Horses could find fame this year.

Just a couple of points to bear in mind. The odd thing about being boss of the year is that although you're the star of the show, you don't get everything you want, or think you want. Being in charge brings responsibilities as well as privileges. And when you get to do things 100 per cent your own way, there's no one to blame if *your way* turns out to include mistakes you hadn't foreseen.

What's more, when you're allowed to be completely yourself with no one to hold you back or modify your behaviour, you might find your obviously very minor, more or less minuscule, almost imperceptible, faults suddenly burst out, magnified and unstoppable at the worst possible moments.

The combination of fire on fire could cause many a Horse to get overheated and overemotional, or storm off in a rage just when they should have been calm and reasonable. Yet letting rip with a strop could torpedo many a promising opportunity this year, Horse.

Then there's the carefree Horse attitude to money. Most Horses pride themselves on not being mercenary, penny-pinching types; they like to spend and have a good time with their horsey mates. And there is nothing wrong with that. But this year, despite the rewards from your career success flowing in, it's even easier than usual to burn through the lot.

Will you even care? Probably not, Horse, because all in all, you're going to have a ball!

The Wonder of Being a Horse
No need to be modest, Horse; you've always known you were gorgeous.

Even if you're not conventionally good-looking, you're blessed with a strong, healthy physique, thick glossy hair, and large, expressive eyes. Always striking, you're admired wherever you go.

In China, the Horse is believed to be a symbol of power, speed, and freedom. People born in the year of the Horse exude a similar magnificence and independence of spirit. Yet they're often misunderstood by other signs. The rest of the zodiac sees that the Horse is a herd animal and also notices that people born under this sign are wonderfully gregarious. Zodiac Horses love to be surrounded by friends, enjoying social occasions or partying, and will grab any chance for a chat. So, the rest of the zodiac puts two and two together and makes twenty-two.

Add to this the Horse's penchant for frequent grooming – they love having their hair brushed, nails beautified, or their feet massaged - and they think they've got you sussed, Horse.

Which is why it can come as a shock when they discover there's a lot more to you than first meets the eye.

For a start, though you love having your gang around you, the typical Horse also requires a lot of 'me time'. The urge to be free is very strong, and when people or situations seem to press too close, the Horse instinct is to race for the hills, metaphorically speaking. One minute, the Horse is there; the next, they've gone and will disappear alone for hours on end, often with no explanation.

The other trait that surprises non-Horses is that despite the wonderful physical strength and courage of the typical Horse, their nerves are very close to the surface. Loud noises, aggressive situations, worrying events, or sudden shocks upset them far more than seems necessary.

Though the brave Horse will attempt to hide the feelings of panic that sweep over them when unfortunate incidents occur, they often come across as moody and difficult as a result.

What's more, the Horse can be a little temperamental. It's mainly because the typical Horse has so much energy and vitality, other signs just can't keep up, and Horse gets impatient. But, also, the typical Horse tends to change its mind quite frequently, which can be annoying for other signs.

And then there's the way Horse can suddenly overreact to an innocent remark that no one else finds offensive. This has more to do with the Horse's love of drama than genuinely hurt feelings. Just occasionally, Horse will throw a moody simply to stir things up and see what happens.

Nobody's perfect, of course, and despite their little foibles, the typical Horse is popular and friendly. They do well at work. As smart and attractive employees, those in authority like having Horse on their staff. The Horse will work hard and charm everyone, yet may not stay around for long. The typical Horse has a habit of starting a job with great enthusiasm but then quickly getting bored. Just when everything seems to be going well, Horse will suddenly up and leave, and pay raises or promises of promotion are unlikely to change the Horse mind. The lure of pastures new is just too strong to resist.

The Horse Home

The thing about the Horse home is that Horse isn't often in it. Home is where Horse keeps its 'stuff' and also goes to sleep or unwind.

The rest of the time, the Horse likes to be out. Horse loves to entertain – and the more friends or family, the merrier – but reckons the nearest pub or restaurant makes the ideal setting for the get-together.

Visitors are most likely to enter the Horse home just briefly, when picking Horse up en-route to the next adventure. They are likely to trip over the odd dog or two, various discarded trainers, or items of sports equipment. Further inside, the furnishings tend to be comfortable and well-worn, enlivened by various practical gadgets in the kitchen and living room, and shelves groaning with grooming aids in the bathroom.

In fact, the typical Horse home is functional, catering perfectly to Horse's needs and bare of unnecessary fripperies like scatter cushions and pot plants. Just the way Horse likes it, in fact.

Being Friends with the Horse

It's not difficult to strike up a friendship with the typical Horse. Horse is usually friendly, charming, and ready to be sociable. Just don't expect to be an exclusive bestie – Horse has nothing against besties, but can't see the point of confining itself to just one or two. The Horse prefers to recruit an ever-changing number of special mates.

Despite this, the Horse is good company as long as you can keep up. The typical equine bores easily and needs constant changes of scenery, preferably with some physical activity thrown in.

Horse will want to round up the gang to go rock-climbing, jogging, or maybe paintballing, attend sports events or camp out at the latest festival. And if there's a competitive element involved, so much the better. Life with Horse is never dull.

Yet, be prepared for the jovial Horse to suddenly take offence at some tiny remark and stomp off in a huff. The tantrum doesn't last long and Horse usually returns later as if nothing happened. The truth is Horse feelings are not as robust as Horse pretends, and can be bruised easily by the most inadvertent and unintentional comment.

Horse Superpowers
Vibrant energy

Infectious enthusiasm

Youthful charm

Best Jobs for Horse 2026
Marketing

Public Relations

Travel Agent

Pet Therapist

Sports Coach

Perfect Partners
Cupid's arrow can strike anywhere at any time, of course, but once the novelty of new romance wears off, some relationships are easier to maintain than others. Here's a guide to the Horse's compatibility with other signs.

Horse with Horse

No doubt about it, these two make a magnificent couple, and any foals in the family would be spectacular. They certainly understand each other, particularly their shared need for both company and alone time, so in general, they get on well. The only tricky part could come if they both grew anxious over the same issue at the same time. Neither would find it easy to calm the other.

Horse with Goat

Goat and Horse just click! These two love kicking up their heels and trotting off into the green. Goat doesn't need to go far or do anything strenuous but is always up for a break in routine, while Horse doesn't do routine at all, so is constantly on the lookout for a partner ready to escape. This couple rarely considers the consequences but, mostly, they don't need to.

Horse with Monkey

Uh oh – best not attempted unless it's love at first sight. Monkey and Horse have wildly different outlooks and can't seem to see eye to eye on anything. They're both lively but in different ways that don't complement each other. Monkey will consider Horse's moods illogical and pointless, while Horse is irritated that Monkey makes no attempt to understand how Horse feels. Very hard work.

Horse with Rooster

The eye-catching Rooster intrigues Horse while Rooster appreciates Horse's strength and agility. They can enjoy many stimulating dates together. Yet, in the long run, this couple may not be able to provide the stability the other needs. They're both sensitive types but in different ways. After a while, the relationship could run out of steam.

Horse with Dog

Both good friends of man, these two can make a formidable team. Dog understands the occasional need for solitude while admiring Horse's strength and agility. Horse, meanwhile, senses Dog's loyalty and down-to-earth nature. Both lovers of the great outdoors and physical activity, they'll never be short of adventures to share. A promising long-term relationship.

Horse with Pig

Pig and Horse are good companions. Horse is soothed by easy-going Pig, and Pig is proud to be seen with such an alluring creature as Horse. They don't have a lot of interests in common, but they don't antagonise each other either. They can jog along amicably for quite a while, but in the long term, they may find they each want more than the other can provide.

Horse with Rat

Rat and Horse both fizz with energy, and they love action and looking good, yet this is not seen as an ideal partnership. Nothing's impossible, of course, but these two will have to work hard to find harmony. The Rat will admire Horse's enthusiasm and cheerful approach but become impatient to discover Horse can also be fiery and emotional. Horse, on the other hand, can find Rat's risk-taking behaviour extremely worrying.

Horse with Ox

Long ago on many Western farms, Ox was replaced by the Horse, and it may be that Ox has never forgotten and never forgiven. At any rate, these two – despite both being big, strong animals – are not usually friends. Horse is too flighty and frivolous to interest Ox for long, while Ox's methodical, careful ways will irritate the Horse. Best not to go there.

Horse with Tiger

This athletic pair gets on pretty well. They both like physical pursuits, testing their strength out of doors or just enjoying the feel of the wind in their hair and the ground under their feet. True, Horse may not quite understand Tiger's plans for world domination, but it doesn't really matter. Horse is happy to be loyal to such a charismatic partner. As they're both moody, there could be rows, but making up is exciting.

Horse with Rabbit

This could be tricky. It's fairly unlikely that Horse and Rabbit would ever end up on a date, but if they did and there was a strong attraction, it could lead to a love/hate relationship. Rabbit's neat and tidy ways would enrage Horse, and Horse's unpredictable moods and over-the-top reactions would annoy Rabbit. Soon, Horse is likely to bolt for the hills or Rabbit retreat to its burrow.

Horse with Dragon

The athletic Horse is pretty good at keeping up with the dashing Dragon. And Dragon appreciates a partner who enjoys getting out and about as much as Dragon does. Yet Horse might grow weary of Dragon's constant new projects and resent having to be involved. Horse likes to go off and do Horsey things at frequent intervals, which Dragon tends to view as disloyal. This relationship could get fiery.

Horse with Snake

At some level, perhaps Horse remembers how Snake beat him in the calendar race, so despite an initial attraction, these two could be wary of each other. Snake is impressed by Horse's energy and athleticism, while Horse admires Snake's elegance and charm. Yet they don't really have much in common. Deep thinking Snake could find Horse rather shallow, and Horse may see Snake as frustratingly enigmatic.

Horse Love 2026 Style

This could be a thrilling year, Horse. Romantically speaking. You adore drama, passion, and tempestuous emotions, and in 2026 you'll be drenched in the lot – often at the same time. You're so alluring, so hot right now, other signs are in danger of getting burned just by stepping too close, like helpless moths to a candle flame. And flirty fillies are particularly risky for them.

In Japan, the woman born under the sign of the Horse is reckoned to be so headstrong, she'll end up being the death of her long-suffering husband. Only an old superstition, of course, but there's definitely a whiff of the 'femme fatale' about quite a few female Horses this year.

Single Horses will enjoy themselves enormously. As besotted admirers try to cling to their sleeves, the Single Horse can brush them off, with a toss of their gorgeous mane, insisting you can't pin down a free spirit, as they gallop away to the next conquest.

Attached Horses can look forward to either a marriage or a split, with the possibility that whichever option they choose will be reversed before the year's out. Rows, tantrums, passionate interludes, break-ups, make-ups – onlookers can't cope – but the feisty Horse relishes it all.

Secrets of Success in 2026

In theory, Horse, all you need to do is turn up, and everything you touch should turn to gold. It's your year after all, so everyone should *do as you say*, shouldn't they? What's not to like?

Well, leaving aside the mistaken belief that everyone will do as you say (they won't!), the main problem you're likely to encounter this year is yourself, Horse!

It's great you've got your confidence back and wonderful the way everyone seems to admire you and think your ideas are genius. But there is such a thing as overconfidence, and it's a trap many a horse could fall into this year. After a while, with things going so well, it wouldn't be surprising if you began to take your good fortune for granted. You're in danger of getting a little slapdash, of believing that since it's your year, you don't need to put in so much effort. Not much point in being the boss if you can't put your feet up now and then, right? Wrong!

Then there's that impatient streak of yours, Horse. Very minor, of course, but you must admit you can get a bit snappy now and then when things move too slowly. This year, with all that extra fire racing through your veins, patience could be in short supply. You could find yourself losing your cool where once you'd have bitten your tongue. You'll either end up having a row with someone who needed handling with kid gloves, or you'll storm off in a rage. Neither approach will do you any favours.

In 2026, your emotions are going to be flaming closer to the surface than usual and the urge to rip up anything that isn't working perfectly and start again, will be very strong. But stay professional, count to ten very slowly when provoked, think diplomacy at all times, and you'll create a fabulous year.

The Horse Year at a Glance

January – Horsey jitters are getting to you. You can sense things are changing, and it is hard to sit still. A daily jog might calm things down.

February – Hallelujah, your year has arrived! Drape yourself in lucky red and get out there and party.

March – A picky person at work is unusually cooperative. Is it a one-off, or is your 2026 magic working? Who cares. Make the most.

April – The boss suddenly recognises your gifts. More responsibility could be coming your way. Not a problem for efficient Horse.

May – Your success is upsetting the Green Eyed Monster. A jealous colleague tries to stir things up.

June – Choppy waters have been averted; you can relax and enjoy yourself.

July – Always a good month for a Horsey holiday. A like-minded friend has a novel idea.

August – A fascinating stranger catches your eye. Not your usual type, but might be fun to explore.

September – You've been called in to assist; it could be a colleague or someone in the family circle. You don't have much time to spare, but do your best.

October – An admirer surprises you. You always suspected they might be secretly smitten, but now it's out in the open.

November – Now this is more like it. A big excuse for shopping and more shopping! Chances are, the boss is so pleased with you that you get a day off for a spree.

December – It looks like you'll be away for Christmas or at least letting someone else do the cooking. Equine bliss.

Lucky colours for 2026: Red, Pink, Green

Lucky numbers for 2026: 6, 8, 9

Three Takeaways

Stay cool

Count to ten before you act

Not everything's about you

CHAPTER 3: THE GOAT

Goat Years

17 February 1931 – 5 February 1932

5 February 1943 – 24 January 1944

24 January 1955 – 11 February 1956

9 February 1967 – 29 January 1968

28 January 1979 – 15 February 1980

15 February 1991 – 3 February 1992

1 February 2003 – 21 January 2004

19 February 2015 – 7 February 2016

6 February 2027 – 25 January 2028

24 January 2039 – 11 February 2040

11 February 2051 – January 31 2052

Natural Element: Fire

Will 2026 be a Glorious Year for the Goat?

It just keeps getting better and better, Goat. Splash out on that colourful outfit you've been eyeing, pour yourself a celebratory beverage, and get ready to enjoy your best year for quite a while, in perfect Goat style.

If you're typical of your sign, Goat, 2024 under the not-so-tender-care of the Dragon, wore you out, and while last year (organised by the more restrained Snake) was an improvement, it wasn't without its stresses. It is not surprising, then, if you approach 2026 with a certain wariness. What now, many a Goat might be thinking. Are we talking fight or flight here?

Well, the good news, Goat, is it's neither! We're talking a very promising year filled with all sorts of Goaty delights. Far from running away, you'll probably want to hang around and hope 2026 lasts a bit longer. This pleasing situation is all thanks to the new ruler of the year – the magnificent Horse – a sign that just happens to be your *very good friend*. Possibly your very best friend, in fact.

As Horse's beloved bestie, you're going to benefit for 12 whole months, from helping hands arriving fortuitously whenever you need them, and good fortune and lucky breaks crossing your path wherever you go.

This is because you and Horse are both Fire creatures, so you just 'get' each other without even trying. Even though Horse is a bit more flamboyant and energetic than you are, Goat, it doesn't matter. You make allowances for each other's different constitutions and trot along happily together.

Horse has always thought a lot of you, Goat, and reckons you tend to be underestimated. This year, then, you could be astonished to find your talents suddenly recognised in an unexpected manner. If you're typical of your sign, you tend to work away conscientiously, getting the job done as thoroughly as possible, regardless of the reward. And because you don't make a big deal of it, your efforts are not always as appreciated as they should be.

Well, not this year Goat. This is the year you're destined to make your name, and for some Goats, it will be in a big way. If you happen to work in a creative or artistic field, you could even end up famous!

Quite a few signs moved house during the year of the Snake, inspired by the Snake's penchant for skin shedding and starting anew, and many Goats were among them. But if, for some reason, you didn't make the move in 2025, Goat, it looks like you'll be taking the plunge this year.

Goats who did move and are now acclimatising to their new pastures will find that they really begin to settle in 2026. Friendly new neighbours start knocking on your door, relatives may relocate near you, community projects beckon, and without consciously making an effort, you could find yourself becoming a prominent figure in the neighbourhood by the end of the year. There could even be gentle pressure to accept some political responsibility or at least represent the interests of the community in some way.

Normally, such an idea would be unthinkable to modest Goat, but with the Fire year boosting your confidence sky-high, you might just be persuaded to accept. You never know, Goat, you could be running the whole country before long!

Goats that didn't manage to find a new place last year are quite likely to stumble across the perfect pad when they least expect it… when they're actually busy with another project totally unconnected to house hunting. Don't worry, this lucky find is just meant for you.

If you're typical of your sign, Goat, you're not particularly driven by money. Yet last year's Snake oversaw a steady stabilising of the Goat finances, and your success at work this year should ensure a pleasing boost to swell them further.

Business Goats, in particular, will also do very well as long as they don't let their enthusiasm run away with them. The general air of optimism and confidence swirling around you at the moment could lead you to waste time and money on a project so risky that other signs might call it madness. Even with the Horse's good fortune on your side, there are some ventures that don't have a hope. Steer clear.

Yet, for all the excitement around your career and artistic hobbies, the area of your life that gives you the most pleasure, Goat, is probably your family and friends. And, in 2026, you are extra blessed. In recent years, many Goats have been secretly saddened to find themselves further from their loved ones than they wanted to be. As a herd animal, there's nothing the typical Goat likes better than to be surrounded by their own gang, including ideally, a whole bunch of boisterous kids.

Yet, lately, circumstances forced many a Goat family apart. Fortunately, the Horse, another herd animal, understands exactly how you feel and is creating the right conditions to bring you all back together again.

Many Goats will be delighted to find close and even extended family members are suddenly noticing how delightful Goat's area has become and making plans to join you. Old friends could follow suit, and you may soon be the centre of a large and expanding social circle.

Other Goats could end up actually hosting family or friends in their own home, possibly permanently. This could be tricky at first, Goat, but chances are you'll learn to love the arrangement. And this year, it looks as if you'll be planning some huge, exciting get-together where the whole clan takes off together to have fun in the sun.

The Wonder of Being a Goat

You've always been the modest type, Goat, that's obvious, but you really have to accept you're unique. There's no one quite like you, and that's just a fact. What's more, even though you never push yourself forward, if you're typical of your sign, other signs seem to know this instinctively. Goats are usually treated with respect wherever they go, despite their unassuming manner.

The Goat modesty is puzzling at first since the live animal is famously sure-footed. And, in fact, despite their diffident appearance, the typical zodiac Goat rarely puts a foot wrong. Maybe their apparent lack of confidence is down to a certain confusion over their identity in the world. To this day, some authorities know the sign as the Sheep. Others, in more macho style, have it down as the Ram. But, either way, there's a certain ambiguity about Goat's energy.

The confusion seems to stem from different translations of the original Chinese word back in the mists of time. But what's in a name, after all? The important point is that whether you're called Goat, Sheep, or Ram, we're talking about a sign that symbolises the beautiful qualities of peace and harmony. Not only that, it's the eighth sign of the zodiac, and according to Chinese lore, the number eight is believed to be a lucky number and associated with growth and prosperity.

So, the Goat has every reason to be proud. And it turns out that although this gentle sign would rather avoid conflict wherever possible, it's not the pushover that more aggressive types might assume.

Back the Goat into a corner, and bullies will be amazed at the feisty response. This is a Fire creature, after all, and when pushed too far, the Goat temper can suddenly burst into flames. Too late, the bully may remember that real live Goats have sharp horns for a reason and know how to use them.

Most of the time, of course, people born in a Goat year are known as the sweetest and friendliest of signs. They are tolerant and kind, have no wish to be competitive, and want to see the best in everyone they meet.

They are so agreeable in fact, no one notices that the Goat usually ends up doing exactly what it pleases. Deep down, the Goat is quietly stubborn, and once it's made up its mind, it rarely changes it. The great thing about the Goat, though, is that it has no wish to force others to agree. It will happily go it alone with whatever course of action it decides upon. You can join Goat or abstain as you wish; the Goat is perfectly content either way but nothing will deter it from its chosen path.

Yet despite their laid-back exterior, few Goats are as calm as they appear. Conflict, harsh words, and stressful situations upset them deeply, and they will worry silently for weeks until all is resolved.

The typical Goat adores lovely things and sees beauty all around in the most unlikely of objects. They're not naturally materialistic and view money merely as a useful tool to create the lifestyle they prefer. And we're not talking vast mansions, designer clothes, or fancy cars here.

An attractive home, a pretty garden, and a characterful run-around to get them where they want to go if they're too far from a bus route will suit the typical Goat just fine, as long as they've also got time to enjoy the things they enjoy.

Most Goats are born artistic. Many have some wonderful talent that takes them far, but even the Goats who can't paint, sculpt, design or write songs tend to have an eye for colour and proportion and an ever-changing list of crafts they're dying to try. The true Goat is rarely bored.

The Goat home

The typical Goat home tends to captivate visitors. They're charmed and surprised because – whether it's a tiny flat, modest cottage, or spacious villa – it somehow manages to exude a quirky vibe that's both homely and stylish at the same time.

Goat pays no attention to fashion and is not interested in status symbols or trying to impress. Yet, the Goat's natural artistic flair ensures that no matter how they throw unlikely objects together, everything settles miraculously and in perfect harmony.

Every Goat home is unique because the typical Goat has little interest in chain stores and mass-produced furnishings. Instead, Goat prefers to potter from junk shop to car boot sale, from charity outlet to auction house, gathering unusual treasures as they go. Goat has even been known to rescue unloved items from abandoned skips. And, of course, each precious find has to be allocated a new berth, chez Goat. Too big, too small? No problem. Goat is the master or mistress of upcycling and reworking.

The resulting collection of mismatched and reimagined objects shouldn't work, but thanks to Goat's talents, it does. Eclectic is the word for the typical Goat home decor style. Many visitors have tried to recreate the effect, but none succeed. That's the genius of the Goat.

Being Friends with the Goat

It's not difficult to be friends with the Goat. Amiable and easy-going, the Goat gets on with almost everyone. Few ever fall out with the equable Goat. In fact, the Goat is so unsettled by cross words and conflict that it will frequently wear itself out acting as peacemaker between warring parties.

The Goat is also highly undemanding. Should you wish to accompany Goat on some Goaty expedition – most likely to some art sale or restoration yard – Goat is delighted to have your company. But if it's not your thing, Goat totally understands and will happily go alone.

The only potential problem is that Goat expects friends to be equally undemanding. If your chosen entertainment is not appealing to Goat, Goat sees nothing amiss in saying 'no thank you'. So, should you require a friend who will drop everything to keep you company, Goat is possibly not the best choice. Clingy, needy types are too stressful for the Goat constitution.

Then again, the Goat can often turn stubborn over some apparently small, insignificant detail and refuse to budge, even when their position seems unreasonable and not in their best interests. No point trying to talk them around. You just have to accept their point of view and move on.

Goat Superpowers
Tenacity

Creativity

Self-Reliance

Best Jobs for Goat 2026
Play Coordinator

Paediatrician

Counsellor

Interior Designer

Therapist

Charity Worker

Perfect Partners
Cupid's arrow can strike anywhere at any time, of course, but once the novelty of new romance wears off, some relationships are easier to maintain than others. Here's a guide to the Goat's compatibility with other signs.

Goat with Goat

When things are going well, you won't find a happier couple than two Goats. They are perfectly in tune with each other's creative natures and understand when to do things together and when to step back and give the other space. And since they both share the same interests, their together times are always fun. Yet, when practical problems arise, neither can easily cope. With a helpful friend on speed dial, this would work.

Goat with Monkey

Monkey and Goat are different, but in a good way. Though they don't quite 'get' each other deep down, Goat admires Monkey's lively personality and magical ability to come up with solutions for everything, while curious Monkey enjoys Goat's knowledge of the arts and the unusual. Long-term, Goat might not present enough of a challenge for Monkey but, with effort, it's a promising match.

Goat with Rooster

Peaceful Goat is not one to make feathers fly, so these two are unlikely to fall out, but they're unlikely to find perfect compatibility, either. Goat is unable to give Rooster the regular ego boosts that make Rooster thrive, while Rooster is baffled by Goat's unpredictable devotion to impractical projects or people. Misunderstandings are likely.

Goat with Dog

This is another relationship that could be tricky. Loyal Dog would be quite willing to stand by Goat when practical problems loom but could end up irritated by Goat's inability to learn from previous mistakes and so keeps making them. Goat can't understand why Dog gets so bothered. With care, these two could learn to live together.

Goat with Pig

Happy-go-lucky Pig and laid-back Goat make a good pair. They hate to stir up trouble and always look for a peaceful solution to any challenge. Ideally, they'd avoid the challenge altogether. They could be very contented together as long as Pig's spending and Goat's inability to deal with finances doesn't get them into trouble.

Goat with Rat

The Rat is charmed by carefree Goat and fascinated by its artistic talent and happy knack of living in the present. Easy-going Goat tends to like everyone, so is perfectly content to enjoy Rat's company. These two can get along fine, yet they don't really understand each other deep down. Long-term, the Rat may find Goat's lack of interest in the practical side of life irritating.

Goat with Ox

Though these two share artistic natures (even if in the case of the Ox, they're well hidden), deep down they don't 'get' one another. Ox may be beguiled at first by Goat's friendly, easy-going manner but then disappointed to discover Goat seems to find everyone equally delightful, even those who are plainly unworthy. Goat, on the other hand, can't understand why Ox won't lighten up more. This relationship would require a lot of effort and compromise.

Goat with Tiger

Tiger and Goat don't have a lot in common. While their aims and temperaments are quite different, they are both sociable creatures, and Goat wouldn't mind Tiger attracting all the attention when they're out together. Tiger, in return, would appreciate Goat's lack of jealousy and generosity of spirit. Yet, in the long-term, they're likely to drift apart as they follow their different interests.

Goat with Rabbit

Wow! One glance across a crowded room, and that's it for Goat and Rabbit. Rabbit instantly recognises and appreciates Goat's innate style and authenticity, while Goat admires Rabbit's restrained elegance and understated intellect. Both are quiet, home-loving types; they also adore exploring and acquiring fine things. This couple will never be bored.

Goat with Dragon

Goat tends to baffle the busy Dragon. Dragon can see Goat is the creative type but can't understand why Goat doesn't appear to be working very hard when so much could be achieved. In fact, if they stayed together long enough, Dragon could help Goat make the most of many talents, but it's unlikely either of them can sustain enough interest for this to happen.

Goat with Snake

Snake and Goat could enjoy many happy hours touring art galleries and exhibitions together. Neither of them craves excitement and harsh, adrenaline-boosting activities, and both appreciate creative, artistic personalities. There's no pressure to compete with each other, so these two would sail along quite contentedly. Not a passionate alliance, but they could be happy.

Goat with Horse

Goat and Horse just click! These two love kicking up their heels and trotting off into the green. Goat doesn't need to go far or do anything strenuous but is always up for a break in routine, while Horse doesn't do routine at all, so is constantly on the lookout for a partner ready to escape. This couple rarely considers the consequences, but mostly, they don't need to.

Goat Love 2026 Style

This could be your summer of love, Goat. You may not think of yourself as the most sensual and seductive of signs, but that's only because you're so modest! Under that bashful exterior, you're smouldering hot, and the other signs can sense it. You're a fire creature after all, Goat, and this Fire year, the temperature around you is rising so fast, lovestruck bystanders could get singed.

Your dazzling aura attracts so many admirers in 2026 that you may not know how to handle them. Trouble is, as a sensitive Goat, you hate to hurt people's feelings or disappoint them, but be realistic – you just can't date them all! Once you learn how to say no, diplomatically, you can relax and have a ball.

Single Goats will certainly enjoy more than their fair share of romance, but don't chop and change too much. Variety is the spice of life, of course, but amongst all those adoring fans, there could well be someone special. Audition as many as you like, Goat, but keep an eye out for your soulmate. They could well turn up any time now.

Attached Goats are promised a contented year. Just watch out that your partner doesn't start resenting all the attention you're attracting, and you'll be fine. Keep the peace, and the two of you will delight in a blissful year of fun with the family.

Secrets of Success in 2026

As a non-mercenary sign with many other interests besides making money, your idea of success could be regarded as eccentric by other signs, Goat. In fact, chances are, you don't really aim for success at all. All you want to do is complete whatever you're working on, and as perfectly as you possibly can. Each project would be a mini masterpiece if you had your way.

So, this year, while the Horse doesn't fully understand *why* you have to polish up every detail quite so thoroughly, Goat, beneficial energy will waft your projects to a wonderful conclusion. What's more, for once, your efforts will be appreciated on a grand scale. Success will find you, Goat, no matter how you try to hide.

Basically, all you have to do is keep on doing what you do, and you can't fail!

Yet the outlook isn't completely perfect. All that fire will give you plenty of energy, Goat, and you're on course to get far more done than usual. But though physically you're the toughest of creatures, and your modest frame conceals surprising stamina, you're sometimes too sensitive for your own good. The same fiery atmosphere that invigorates you so much can have an unfortunate effect on the people around you.

Suddenly, you're running into arguments or aggressive behaviour. People who are normally reasonable and accommodating can turn truculent and moody. Many a Goat finds this so upsetting that they abandon whatever they were working on and withdraw, hurt, which is a shame. How many possibly brilliant ideas were thrown away before their potential could be realised, Goat? All because you got stressed?

So, this year, walk away the second conflict threatens. Close your ears to heated words or at least refuse to take them personally. Remember, they're not really aimed at you. It's just a passing storm. Rise above the turbulence and claim the fabulous year you deserve.

The Goat Year at a Glance

January – A new idea forms at the back of your mind. You could be onto something exciting.

February – The weather's still grim, but you perceive a brightening in the atmosphere. People are starting to take you seriously, Goat.

March – A new face in the workplace only has eyes for you, Goat. Watch out if you're attached, but for single Goats things could get interesting.

April – An avalanche of work falls your way, Goat. You can cope. One step at a time.

May – A rest would be nice, and now it looks like you might get a break. Your efforts last month have been noticed.

June – The boss wants to see you, but don't worry, it's good news. Promotion beckons.

July – Parties galore. You can't attend them all… or can you? Dig out those dancing shoes, Goat.

August – Someone in your circle is organising a big family getaway. Right up your street, Goat. You drop everything to help.

September – a prickly person could upset you. Don't let them get to you, Goat. They don't even mean it.

October – Work gets busy again, but a stickler for the rules tries to slow you down. Good thing you're the kind, patient type, Goat.

November – Suddenly, everyone's fixated on food. Early feasting, and restaurant meet-ups everywhere you look. Forget the diet and dig in.

December – First Christmas in your new home? Even if it's not, you transform it with your festive creations. A magical time.

Lucky colours for 2026: Pink, Apple Green, Magenta

Lucky numbers for 2026: 3, 4, 9

Three Takeaways

Time to be Bold
Ignore the mean critics
Follow your instincts

CHAPTER 4: THE MONKEY

Monkey Years

6 February 1932 – 25 January 1933

25 January 1944 – 12 February 1945

12 February 1956 – 30 January 1957

30 January 1968 – 16 February 1969

16 February 1980 – 4 February 1981

4 February 1992 – 22 January 1993

22 January 2004 – 8 February 2005

8 February 2016 – 27 January 2017

26 January 2028 – 12 February 2029

12 February 2040 – 31 January 2041

1 February 2052 – 18 February 2053

Natural Element: Metal

Will 2026 be a Glorious Year for the Monkey?

Time to start limbering up, Monkey. 2026 looks like it will be an amazing year for you. Not necessarily easy, but overflowing with opportunities for the clever Monkey to grab and leap speedily away with. Yet to make the most, you need to be at your leanest, fittest, and most focused.

Last year probably proved demanding for quite a few Monkeys. It could have been difficult to attract the attention you needed, or harder than usual to get your ideas taken seriously.

You didn't do anything wrong, Monkey. It's just that you and the Snake ruler of 2025 aren't exactly best buddies. Not that you've fallen out, it's simply that the two of you have never had anything in common. You're so very different in every way, there's almost no point of contact. So, any beneficial luck on offer tended to go to signs more favoured by the serpent. Poor Monkeys were last in the queue.

Yet if you're typical of your sign, you weren't fazed one bit. With the Monkey genius for improvisation and lateral thinking, you simply performed a metaphorical double somersault and achieved your aims in a different way.

Well, you'll be glad to hear that 2026 is quite different, Monkey. It's not that you and the Horse are tremendous besties. You're not. You still don't 'get' each other on many levels. But the great thing about Horse energy is that it's strong and vital and so obviously going places; you can't help but be inspired. The one thing lively Monkey can't bear is to be bored, and Horse is never boring.

So, this year, the fiery atmosphere will fill you with burning ambition. A sudden restlessness with the same old *same old*, could see many a Monkey abandoning their former career and reaching for the stars in a totally different field. Since the typical Monkey is so versatile and multi-talented, this is unlikely to be a problem. Very soon, you'll have cracked the new role and be well on the way to success.

Business Monkeys also want to branch out and are beguiled by the seductive possibilities of AI. Unravelling the intricacies of new technology will keep you happy for months, Monkey.

But the main thing to remember is that everything is happening with breathtaking speed. We're talking Racehorse here, Monkey. The Crimson Horse, the swiftest of the herd, can cover the ground like a raging inferno. Opportunities will fly your way so fast that even the agile Monkey's reflexes will barely manage to react in time. Yet for the Monkeys that do, there are rich rewards.

As a Metal creature, you have a natural way with money, Monkey. Money seeks you out and you seldom end up in serious financial trouble. What's more, while you're not in any way mean, you have a clever knack of discovering discounts and devising ingenious methods of leveraging your cash so a little goes a long way. Plenty of windfalls will waft in your direction courtesy of the Horse this year, Monkey, but with so much fire blazing around, you're likely to burn through more than usual.

Some of that spending could be a result of your travel plans. While always in search of variety, the typical Monkey often finds it quite close to home. This year, though, under the adventurous influence of the

Horse, many a Monkey will be travelling far and wide. It won't be cheap, but you're going to love every minute.

It's very likely that work and travel will intertwine, too. Quite a few Monkeys could even be drawn to new careers in the travel industry. Ever fancied running a hotel or a tourist attraction, Monkey? Well, if you didn't before, this could well be the year it suddenly appeals. 'Go Ape' could have been created for you! Maybe you'll go off and devise something similar.

Possibly one of the most demanding aspects of the year could be coping with the people in your orbit, Monkey. Personal relationships suddenly have a puzzling, roller-coaster feel to them, at work as well as at home. Suddenly, everyone's a prima donna. Tears, tantrums, dramatic exits, and emotional returns are all on the menu. Blazing rows erupt over nothing at all. On the other hand, the very same temperamental types can suddenly turn smiley and sunny in an instant.

Fortunately, as a quick-witted Monkey, you can navigate the illogical twists and turns and rapidly calm fraught situations with a joke. These entertainer skills will be much in demand this year, Monkey. They'll add to your popularity no end and could even end up earning you a bonus.

The Wonder of Being a Monkey

Wonder is the right word, Monkey. People born under this intriguing sign really are wonders in their own right. In China, the Monkey is associated with justice, intelligence, and sometimes a certain cunning, while in the West, they're also associated with great agility, curiosity, and a mischievous spirit.

Well, basically, zodiac Monkey, that's you. Deep down, you embody all these qualities in varying degrees. Take agility. You may not be a born gymnast, but if you put your mind to it and you're typical of your sign, you find you have a natural flexibility combined with a raw energy that enables you to master any number of physical activities that take your fancy.

The only thing stopping you is a lack of interest. Yet onlookers can tell, simply by the speed of your movements and the dexterity with which you manipulate any item you happen to be using, you're exceptionally deft and nimble.

Then, there's your enquiring mind. The Monkey child is the one that prises open its phone case to see what's inside, empties the contents of the food cupboard into mum's biggest bowl to see how the resulting mixture comes out, and collects snails in the garden to set up a gastropod race.

Adult Monkeys are highly intelligent, but not necessarily in an academic way. They enjoy puzzles, quizzes, and tricky tasks such as assembling intricate flat-pack furniture. They excel at problem-solving of every kind. They also have a strong sense of humour and a weakness for practical jokes that may not appeal to other signs.

Basically, the Monkey needs constant mental stimulation, and when this is in short supply, Monkey's mischievous streak tends to get activated. The resulting mayhem is not usually malicious, simply a way of keeping Monkey entertained, yet these antics often get Monkey into trouble. More awkward still, the Monkey has an instinctive distrust of authority and delights in bending the rules and provoking those in charge. Protesting when caught, it was only a joke, doesn't usually help.

Yet beneath the exterior clown, the Monkey is a great survivor. Most Monkeys know they can afford to play around because they have brainpower to spare. The constant fun and games mask an astute mind with an aptitude for handling money. The Monkey will always do well while apparently not even trying.

The Monkey Home

The phrase most often heard in describing the Monkey home is: 'It'll be nice when it's finished.' The Monkey home is in a constant state of renovation. It's usually a stop-start affair because Monkey tends to begin alterations in a fit of enthusiasm, gets bored, and then takes a break, during which it sees an even better design and resolves to scrap the previous idea to start all over again.

Yet beneath the dust sheets and paint cans, Monkey is likely to have all the latest gadgets and mechanical aids. Anything that can be operated from the Monkey phone, preferably from another continent, will be incorporated whether Monkey needs it or not.

And Monkey is also likely to aspire to a home gym, games room, and maybe even a cinema, should funds permit. Yet, despite all the planned comforts, the typical Monkey often ends up entertaining elsewhere. They just can't abide all that tedious planning and shopping and – in any case – they love a change of scene.

Being Friends with the Monkey

It requires quite a bit of energy and a good sense of humour to be friends with a Monkey. But if you can stand the pace, it's a rewarding relationship. Being around Monkey tends to be a laugh-a-minute affair.

The primate, when in a good mood, loves to entertain and will delight whatever company is around with witty conversation, zany jokes, and crazy ideas. They like to be the centre of attention, too, so if you're not the competitive type and are quite happy to remain the audience, they will appreciate you even more.

They're also active, restless, and can't cope with the same old, same old. They love to explore new haunts, novel entertainments, and exotic foods.

These lively souls need a broad minded, intelligent companion, and you have to be prepared for the odd practical joke which you may not find too funny.

And it's not an entirely undemanding friendship. Monkey can forgive many things but will not stand for being bored. Should the Monkey find you tedious, they'll just melt away.

Monkey Superpowers
Quick wit

Dexterity

Financial wizardry

Best Jobs 2026
Athlete

Entertainer

Linguist

Diplomat

Cryptographer

Event Planner

Perfect Partners
Cupid's arrow can strike anywhere at any time, of course, but once the novelty of new romance wears off, some relationships are easier to maintain than others. Here's a guide to the Monkey compatibility with other signs.

Monkey with Monkey

It's not always the case that opposites attract. More often, like attracts like, and when two Monkeys get together, they find each other delightful. At last, they've met another brain as quick and agile as their own and a person who relishes practical jokes as much as they do. What's more, this is a partner that shares a constant need for change and novelty. Yet, despite this, two Monkeys can often end up competing with each other. As long as they can recognise this, and laugh about it, they'll be fine.

Monkey with Rooster

While not a perfect match, these two have got a lot of time for each other. Monkey recognises the intelligent brain beneath Rooster's plumage, while Rooster admires Monkey's ability to entertain a crowd, and they both adore socialising. They could enjoy many fun dates together. Long-term, though, Rooster may tire of Monkey's jokes.

Monkey with Dog

Monkey finds Dog intriguing. Monkey senses Dog's strength of character coupled with its playful streak, which fits well with Monkey's love of games. Dog, meanwhile, appreciates Monkey's energy and light-hearted approach. Yet, before long, Monkey's disdain for rules will grate on Dog's instinctive love of them. They cannot agree in this area, and it could lead to arguments.

Monkey with Pig

On the surface, these two might seem an unlikely couple. Yet Pig enjoys Monkey's fun and humour while Monkey is happy to be admired uncritically. What's more, Monkey's inventive mind can solve any difficulties caused by Pig's spending, and since Monkey can't resist a challenge, the opportunity to retrain Pig, or at least find a way to obtain purchases cheaper, could help the relationship last.

Monkey with Rat

Unlikely as it might appear, mischievous Monkey and the clever Rat make a good partnership. Their quick minds, sociable natures, and love of novelty ensure that they're never bored together. True, Rat might sometimes feel that Monkey is too inclined to skim over the surface of things and could do with being more serious at times, but Monkey's ingenuity and audaciousness always saves the day. Both can have a weakness for gambling, though, so need to take care.

Monkey with Ox

The naughty Monkey scandalises Ox but in such an amusing way that Ox can't help laughing. Monkey, on the other hand, is equally amused to find an audience that is so easy to shock. This unlikely pair enjoy each other's company and get on surprisingly well. Yet, right from the start, it's probably obvious to both that a long-term relationship couldn't last. A fun flirtation, though, could be a terrific tonic for them both.

Monkey with Tiger

Tiger can't help being intrigued by sparkling Monkey, and Monkey is flattered by such interest. Who wouldn't enjoy being admired by such a fabulous creature? But irrepressible Monkey just can't help teasing, and being teased is not a sensation Tiger is familiar with (or appreciates). Unless the attraction is very strong, these two will wind each other up until they can bear it no longer and part.

Monkey with Rabbit

Mercurial Monkey doesn't really 'get' Rabbit. The Monkey can appreciate how well Rabbit operates and sees that this approach gets good results, but it's all too picky and slow for Monkey. Rabbit, on the other hand, is amused by Monkey's quick wit and clever ways but deplores Monkey's slapdash, sometimes devious tactics. Very unlikely to work out.

Monkey with Dragon

These two are likely to hit it off immediately. Each is attracted to the other's intelligence and lively presence, and Dragon's exuberance doesn't overwhelm hyperactive Monkey. What's more, although they both enjoy being surrounded by a crowd, Monkey only wants to make people laugh, while Dragon hopes to inspire them to a cause. There is no conflict, so this couple can help each other to go far.

Monkey with Snake

These two clever creatures ought to admire each other if only for their fine minds, and at first, it's possible they might. But unless they're really determined to make it work, it won't be long before active Monkey finds Snake's energy-saving ways irritating, while Snake loses patience with Monkey's endless jokes.

Monkey with Horse

Uh oh – best not attempted unless it's love at first sight. Monkey and Horse have wildly different outlooks and can't seem to see eye to eye on anything. They're both lively but in different ways that don't complement each other. Monkey will consider Horse's moods illogical and pointless, while Horse is irritated that Monkey makes no attempt to understand how Horse feels. Very hard work.

Monkey with Goat

Monkey and Goat are different, but in a good way. Though they don't quite 'get' each other deep down, Goat admires Monkey's lively personality and magical ability to come up with solutions for everything, while curious Monkey enjoys Goat's knowledge of the arts and the unusual. Long-term, Goat might not present enough of a challenge for Monkey, but with effort, it's a promising match.

Monkey Love 2026 Style

Well, you just can't fail this year, Monkey. Always the one to light up a room and get everyone gathering around, delighting in your hilarious repartee, you're so charismatic you're on fire right now.

Even if you're not conventionally good-looking, the typical Monkey is devastatingly attractive in a lithe, athletic way. Add this year's fiery atmosphere to your magnetic charm, and other signs are likely to be fighting over you, Monkey.

Normally, you can win over almost any conquest you choose, with your unique social skills, but in 2026, you don't even have to try. You won't have to move a muscle. Just stand there, radiating your natural gorgeousness, and smitten admirers will be at your side in seconds.

Passions are high this year, however, and single Monkeys are likely to arouse strong emotions without even realising it. You're not usually a fan of overt sentimentality, but right now there's a Romeo and Juliet quality about the energy swirling around that mustn't be ignored. *Tread carefully*, Monkey. Enjoy yourself, but don't start a feud.

Attached Monkeys can look forward to exciting travel adventures with their beloved. Hopefully, your partner will share your sudden enthusiasm for exploring. If not, your legendary powers of persuasion should do the trick. Just describe your trips as second honeymoons and fall in love all over again.

Secrets of Success in 2026

Let's look at this a different way, Monkey. What did you do last year that was successful? Okay, so whatever that was, try the opposite this year. Within reason, of course. Don't 'give up' on anything that's currently going well – keep doing it just the way you were if it's working – but *also* look out for something else to do differently.

Where the Snake urged caution, diligence, and attention to detail, the Horse appreciates a grander, broader-brush approach – and that is perfectly in tune with your style, Monkey. It's destiny, you might be saying to yourself! Which it could be, as long as you don't get too carried away. Right now, a tiny flame can suddenly leap into a blazing fire that could twist and incinerate the whole house if you're not careful. Don't let wild enthusiasm blind you to the possible faults of a project. You owe it to yourself to explore all interesting opportunities, but run them by a down-to-earth friend – ideally not another Monkey – before you seal the deal. You don't have to take their advice, but another perspective can help clear your mind. Stick to a 'review it with a friend' policy and it'll be your year, Monkey.

The Monkey Year at a Glance

January – It might be cold outside, but you're still in party mood from the recent festivities. Times are changing, and you're glad.

February – A misery face at work is a bit of a downer, but you're all set for Chinese New Year fun. More parties at your place?

March – Things are still quiet in the workplace, but just as boredom threatens, a new idea strikes.

April – Yay! Someone in authority loves your novel suggestions. You get the go-ahead you wanted.

May – Uh oh. A jealous rival tries to muscle in. You won't stand for it, but play it smart. Think strategy, not open conflict.

June – Suddenly, travel shows and holiday sites catch your eye. Time to organise something different. Really different.

July – Your new project is doing well. Cash starts rolling in. Should you spend or save for that special trip?

August – The boss is so pleased, you're sent to teach the others. Not all of them are close by. Rail and road trips beckon.

September – So much to do, but Monkey always finds time for fun. A smitten admirer only has eyes for you.

October – An unexpected bill may spoil a few plans. Don't worry, Monkey, you'll figure out a cunning solution.

November – A winter wonderland break is on offer. Are you too busy? Are you crazy, Monkey? Go for it.

December – Well done, Monkey. You've made it through to Christmas in terrific form. Celebrate.

Lucky colours for 2026: Flame, Black, Silver

Lucky numbers for 2026: 1, 3, 7

Three Takeaways

Think Big
Steer clear of rows
Don't bend the rules

CHAPTER 5: THE ROOSTER

Rooster Years
26 January 1933 – 13 February 1934
13 February 1945 – 1 February 1946
31 January 1957 – 17 February 1958
17 February 1969 – 5 February 1970
5 February 1981 – 24 January 1982
23 January 1993 – 9 February 1994
9 February 2005 – 28 January 2006
28 January 2017 – 15 February 2018
13 February 2029 – 2 February 2030
1 February 2041 – 21 January 2042
19 February 2053 – 7 February 2054
Natural Element: Metal

Will 2026 be a Golden Year for the Rooster?

Wow, Rooster. Aren't you looking fabulous? You don't think so? Well, think again and stop being so modest! In 2026, love comes looking for you, and you've got romance on your mind. Beauty is in the eye of the beholder, of course, Rooster, but to be on the safe side, make sure your plumage is at its glowing best every time you set foot outside. You're going to get noticed.

Naturally, there are plenty of other goodies in store for Roosters this year, but chances are it's love and then family that will mean the most.

So here you are, Rooster, just emerging from the Year of the Snake, probably with mixed feelings. After the turbulent year of the Dragon in 2024, you were hoping for a quieter time with the Snake of 2025. Well, it looks like many Roosters got their wish, but not in quite the way they hoped. Those who voluntarily slowed down and took things easy were rewarded with a relaxing vibe. But many that resisted and attempted to outrun the soporific Snake were brought to a shuddering halt. Either career issues, health issues, or family responsibilities forced a number of Roosters to take the break they needed.

Yet the odd thing is, despite the apparent setbacks which you probably resented bitterly at the time, chances are you've ended up exactly where you wanted to be all along. How that happened, you're not really sure, but that's the wisdom of the Snake. A good friend with your best interests at heart.

So, if you're typical of your sign, Rooster, you're actually starting the year in a pretty reasonable place, and it's just going to get better and better. The Snake of 2025 was fond of you and looked after you in discreet, understated serpent fashion, but that's nothing compared to the lively affections of the Horse of 2026.

You and the Horse are *best buddies*. Both gregarious, farmyard creatures at heart, despite the difference in scale, and you instinctively look out for each other. So now the Horse has grabbed the reins, equine power will help you make your dreams come true.

For a start, all the Fire that's come galloping in with your four-footed friend has boosted your energy sky high. Roosters with health issues that annoyingly linger from last year will benefit first. Those warming cosmic flames will evaporate aches, pains, and fatigue, and bring your old vitality rushing back.

Roosters whose careers were in the doldrums score next. Suddenly, the confidence to fight back tingles through their veins. The right words, the right attitudes, the right ideas flow effortlessly from their lips, defeating competitors and impressing astonished bosses everywhere.

And finally, Roosters with awkward family members determined to stir up trouble will find that some sort of miracle has occurred. Suddenly, Mr or Mrs Never Satisfied is inspired to go and annoy fresh victims many miles away, leaving you in peace.

As everything falls magically into place, you've now got the time and energy to consider your options, Rooster. Career promotion beckons – your high octane performance has stunned the boss, and as a result, you can pick the role you fancy. Business Rooster has orders flooding in so fast that it's difficult to keep up.

Unexpected refunds, bonuses, and even wins boost the Rooster bank balance. As a metal creature, you've always been good with money and can make it stretch further than most, but now no stretching is required. There's cash to spare.

The outlook's so promising that many a Rooster partner will even suggest relocating the home or business to Rooster's favourite part of the country.

Meanwhile, long-lost or long-estranged friends unexpectedly turn up on the doorstep – all grumbles and disagreements forgotten, wanting to carry on where you last left off.

There's so much on offer, Rooster, and it could seem overwhelming. Yet, with the world apparently at their feet, many Roosters will find they're not so interested in material fripperies after all. What fascinates them right now is love, in all its facets.

If this sounds like you, Rooster, stand by to have your wishes granted. Roosters that felt unappreciated in recent years will suddenly have their value recognised – big time. Prepare to be spoiled, Rooster. So much praise and gratitude is coming your way, you won't stop blushing.

What's more, someone you previously thought of, not exactly as an enemy but certainly not a fan or supporter, will do a complete U-turn. Suddenly, they've changed their opinion from unfavourable to favourable in such a dramatic way, you're speechless. Whether this is at home, in your social circle, or at work, it's going to have far-reaching, beneficial effects on your whole life.

All in all, Rooster, 2026 looks like being an unforgettable year.

The Wonder of Being a Rooster

Well, of course you look wonderful, Rooster. The typical Rooster believes in putting on a good display. You only get one chance at making a first impression after all, as Rooster would say, so it's only sensible to present yourself in the best possible light.

Rooster may live in the cheapest studio flat and survive on a diet of cornflakes and baked beans, but you'd never know it when seeing them strut down the street – striking and coordinated in stylish, flamboyant outfits, usually fizzing with colour.

The Chinese associate the Rooster with courage, and it's easy to see why. The brave farmyard bird will square up to all-comers armed only with a modest beak, a couple of sharp claws, and a piercing shriek. Yet, Rooster is quite prepared to take on the challenge.

People born under the Rooster sign are just as heroic. Though they may be quaking inside and don't seek out conflict, they can't ignore injustice and will wade in on the side of the underdog if they encounter bullying or unfairness.

Sometimes, this tendency gets them into trouble, particularly if they've misjudged the situation, but Rooster remains undaunted and will wade in just as quickly on the next occasion.

Despite misunderstandings, Roosters are popular characters. They're sociable and chatty and love to be surrounded by friends. Admittedly, when lavished with flattering attention, the Rooster raconteur can exaggerate – sometimes wildly – and this can cause embarrassment later when the reality is revealed. But most signs find this trait rather endearing.

The typical Rooster often aspires to be the boss and usually manages it. They're intelligent and organised but sometimes upset employees with an abrasive manner. Roosters tend to forget they need to choose their words with care.

Yet few people realise that, deep down, Rooster lacks confidence. At some level, they feel not quite as good enough as they are, so they have to make up for that lack of confidence with a grand show, hard work, and fearless deeds. For the same reason, their feelings are easily hurt, though the typical Rooster would never admit it.

The Rooster Home

You're unlikely to be invited to a Rooster home should the Rooster be short of funds. Rooster likes to entertain as lavishly as possible and would loathe being unable to ply guests with tasty treats and delightful beverages. When finances permit, though, guests are welcomed to warm rooms that zing with colour and bristle with the latest gadgets. The Rooster is fascinated by clever labour-saving devices and the most up-to-date, super-sleek technology. Where possible, the Rooster home also looks out onto green space of some kind. Although not necessarily keen on gardening, most Roosters retain a trace memory of country living and find the proximity of grass and trees relaxing. The ideal Rooster home boasts bifold doors opening onto a pleasing vista of plants and flowers, even if they live in the centre of town. They particularly enjoy entertaining out of doors, too, and are not put off by a little inclement weather.

Being Friends with the Rooster

The typical Rooster has a wide circle of friends and acquaintances. Outgoing and sociable, they can strike up a new friendship wherever they happen to be. They are excellent company. Great storytellers with long memories, they can enthral listeners with their amusing tales.

Yet the more you know a Rooster, the more layers you discover. For a start, they can be impulsive in actions and also in words. This leads them to speak out more bluntly than is wise… before they've had time to choose the most… ahem… tactful language.

Consequently, the Rooster has a tendency to fall out with people, too. Admittedly, they make new friends as quickly as they lose the old ones, but many Roosters have a confusingly ever-changing network.

What's more, even if you're not bothered by Rooster's occasionally clumsy phrased opinion, Rooster may be bothered by yours. The typical Rooster is surprisingly thin-skinned and can take offence where none was intended.

They find it incredibly easy to misinterpret some innocent remark and will stomp off, deeply wounded by the imagined insult.

The person who understands this is merely a symptom of their feathered friend's lack of confidence will know exactly how to heal Rooster's injured feelings. Manage that and you'll be friends for life.

Rooster Superpowers

Courage

Persistence

Bold action

Best Jobs for Rooster 2026

Model

Dog Trainer

Legal Advisor

Fund Raiser

Therapist

Fashion Designer

Perfect Partners

Cupid's arrow can strike anywhere at any time, of course, but once the novelty of new romance wears off, some relationships are easier to maintain than others. Here's a guide to the Rooster's compatibility with other signs.

Rooster with Rooster

Fabulous to look at, though they would be, these two alpha creatures would find it difficult to share the limelight. They can't help admiring each other at first sight, but since both need to be the boss, there could be endless squabbles for dominance. What's more, neither would be able to give the other the regular reassurance they need. Probably not worth attempting.

Rooster with Dog

Rooster and Dog are not the best of partners. Dog can be as plain-spoken as Rooster and is not likely to be impressed by overt behaviour. Moreover, Dog is often critical, and Rooster can't stand criticism. Rooster, on the other hand, is likely to sense and resent Dog's attitude. Frustration abounds for both in this relationship. Only for the hopelessly love-struck.

Rooster with Pig

These two might seem an unlikely couple – modest Pig with extrovert Rooster. Yet Pig has no need or wish to crow and can see the vulnerable character that lurks beneath Rooster's fine feathers; Rooster, meanwhile, responds to Pig's kindness and undemanding nature. As long as Rooster doesn't get bored, this can be a contented relationship.

Rooster with Rat

The first thing Rat notices about the Rooster is its beautiful plumage, but this is a relationship which is unlikely to get much further than initial admiration. Rooster's direct and frank approach can strike the Rat as tactless, while the Rooster can't understand why Rat has to make life so convoluted and complicated. Then again, Rooster's natural confidence and aplomb can come across as bragging to the Rat. These two have to be very determined to make a partnership work.

Rooster with Ox

For all its bravado and showing off, the Rooster is a down-to-earth type, drawn to security and accumulating the good things in life – requirements that Ox understands very well and can supply effortlessly. What's more, Ox can't help but admire Rooster's fine feathers and skill at communicating in a crowd – attributes Ox doesn't have and is unlikely to acquire. These two could enjoy a very good partnership.

Rooster with Tiger

The only feathered creature in the zodiac, the opulence and novelty of Rooster's appearance will draw Tiger like a magnet. What's more – deep down – they are both quite serious-minded types, so on one level, they'll have much to share. Yet, despite this, they're not really on the same wavelength and misunderstandings will keep recurring. Could be hard work.

Rooster with Rabbit

A difficult match. However unfair it seems, Rooster comes over as loud, boastful, and uncouth to Rabbit, while Rabbit appears dull, staid, and insufficiently admiring of Rooster's fine feathers to appeal to Rooster. These two just can't see below the surface of the other, and it would be surprising if they ended up together. Only to be considered by the very determined.

Rooster with Dragon

A Dragon and Rooster pairing will always attract attention. These two are both gorgeous beings and love to be surrounded by admirers. They will probably enjoy going out together and being seen as a couple, but in the long term, they may not be able to provide the kind of support each secretly needs. Entertaining for a while, but probably not a lasting relationship.

Rooster with Snake

Surprisingly, Snake and Rooster work well together. Both gorgeous in different ways, they complement each other without competing. Snake's keen eyes can see beneath Rooster's proud facade to the sensitive, unsure person inside, while Rooster appreciates Snake's unobtrusive strength and wise words of encouragement at just the right moment. These two could be inseparable.

Rooster with Horse

The eye-catching Rooster intrigues Horse while Rooster appreciates Horse's strength and agility. They can enjoy many stimulating dates together. Yet, in the long run, this couple may not be able to provide the stability the other needs. They're both sensitive types but in different ways. After a while, the relationship could run out of steam.

Rooster with Goat

Peaceful Goat is not one to make feathers fly, so these two are unlikely to fall out, but they're unlikely to find perfect compatibility, either. Goat is unable to give Rooster the regular ego boosts that make Rooster thrive, while Rooster is baffled by Goat's unpredictable devotion to impractical projects or people. Misunderstandings are likely.

Rooster with Monkey

While not a perfect match, these two have got a lot of time for each other. Monkey recognises the intelligent brain beneath Rooster's plumage, while Rooster admires Monkey's ability to entertain a crowd, and they both adore socialising. They could enjoy many fun dates in.

Rooster Love 2026 Style

No question, you're in the mood for love, Rooster. Even better, love's in the mood for you!

Admittedly, you were pretty hot last year, but quite a few Roosters ran into unexpected hitches that ruffled their feathers and put a damper on many a promising dalliance. Well, if that was you, relax. Those hitches have long vanished in the rearview mirror, and now you can make up for lost time. Romance with a capital R is on your mind, and the universe is encouraging you to go for it. The fiery atmosphere of the year adds a special sparkle to your eyes, a lustre to your hair, and lights you up in the most alluring way.

You're positively magnetic right now, Rooster, so check out all those interested faces looking longingly in your direction and decide which one, or three (naughty Rooster!), you fancy drawing into your orbit. All you need to do is give them a sign, and they're yours.

Single Roosters may even find a past love (who didn't treat them as they deserved) comes crawling back, begging forgiveness. Hmm. Should they get a second chance? Up to you, soft-hearted Rooster. Just don't allow a repeat performance.

Attached Roosters can go overboard on creating the perfect love nest. Think soft lights, gentle music, cosy fire crackling in the grate, and a delicious meal warming in the oven. Your partner will be stunned, Rooster. (In a good way!) Add to that a few mini breaks 'a deux' and the two of you'll soon be mistaken for loved-up teenagers.

Secrets of Success in 2026

You probably haven't given much thought to success recently, Rooster. You've had so many other things on your mind. Yet if you're typical of your sign, you did quite well last year when the Snake was in charge. The serpent created quite a few unusual opportunities for farmyard creatures like yourself, and hopefully, you were able to make the most.

This year, the outlook is even better. The blazing fire element is breathing vibrant energy into all your ventures and inspiring you with exciting 'get up and go' ideas. Plus, the Horse is standing by to help race you to wherever you'd like to go.

Yet, despite this, many a Rooster could be hesitating. There are still distracting relationship issues to be sorted. This is because, as well as energising you, the fire element could be having a similar effect on your personal relationships. Suddenly, the people in your orbit are increasingly demanding... but not necessarily in a negative way.

Affectionate friends and loved ones could simply be craving more of your attention.

No point stressing over it, Rooster. Just devise a sensible plan to cope with them. Create a timetable, perhaps. Set aside some dedicated relationship days or hours, and treat those slots the way you'd treat a business meeting (i.e., don't rearrange or postpone when something else comes up).

Once you've sorted out your personal life, Rooster, success is a breeze.

The Rooster Year at a Glance

January – Everyone else has been partying but chances are you've had work to do. And quite a lot of it too. Learn to say no, Rooster.

February – A family member fancies a walk on the wild side. You're sympathetic but can't let them drift too far. Be tactful.

March – An officious type at work wants to reorganise your schedule or mess with the system. You don't have to stand for it.

April – You very seldom crow about your abilities, Rooster, but now you've got something to shout about. Stop being modest! Make sure they all know how brilliant you are.

May – Looks like your talents have been recognised. An interesting offer comes your way.

June – Romance with an artistic type arrives unexpectedly. Where will this lead?

July – Work routines are being shaken up. Could you be relocating or changing jobs altogether?

August – A fun but irresponsible friend tempts you to a festival. Not usually your scene, but life's for living. Just double-check the details before you commit.

September – Yay, looks like a bonus is on the way. Are we talking cash or something metaphorical? Good news either way, Rooster.

October – Think before you speak this month, Rooster. Ultra-sensitive people are itching to take your words the wrong way.

November – Someone you met online wants to meet up in person. Could this be the start of something beautiful?

December – Your circle seems to have expanded hugely over the year, and now they all want to celebrate at yours! Get some help with the cooking, Rooster.

Lucky colours for 2026: Peach, White, Chestnut

Lucky numbers for 2026: 5, 7, 8

Three Takeaways

Fake it till you make it
Just say 'no'
When in doubt, take a break

CHAPTER 6: THE DOG

Dog Years

14 February 1934 – 3 February 1935

2 February 1946 – 21 January 1947

18 February 1958 – 7 February 1959

6 February 1970 – 26 January 1971

25 January 1982 – 12 February 1983

10 February 1994 – 30 January 1995

29 January 2006 – 17 February 2007

16 February 2018 – 4 February 2019

13 February 2029 – 2 February 2030

22 January 2042 – 9 February 2043

8 February 2054 – 27 January 2055

Natural Element: Metal

Will 2026 be a Glorious Year for the Dog?

Now this is more like it, Dog. 2026 could be the year you've been waiting for, for – well, for years! If you're typical of your sign, it's been quite a while since you could say everything's been just peachy for you. It's not even like you ask for much, is it Dog? You're not the greedy type, you don't demand perfection, you don't even ask for more than your fair share. Yet it's probably been so long since the important areas of your life gelled together happily and harmoniously, you can't even remember when it was.

The trouble is, you're a very special, individual character if you're typical of your sign, Dog. This is commendable, but it tends to mean that many of your zodiac cousins just don't understand you. Consequently, when they're in charge of the year, things can go unexpectedly awry.

The pesky Dragon of 2024 somehow oversaw quarrels and unfortunate events in the canine world. Then the Snake of 2025 came along and things improved, but you still kept running into obstacles.

Well, the good news is, at last your *luck has changed.* Here comes the Horse, riding to the rescue, determined to make 2026 something to remember. You and the Horse have always been great mates. Your two namesakes, faithful companions to man more or less since humans began walking the earth, have often worked together, each as indispensable as the other. So, the Horse and the Dog have a lot in common.

You make a great team and this year the Horse will see to it you experience that cosmic teamwork in dynamic action. In day-to-day life, this could take the form of a surprising run of good fortune that ensures everything you do proceeds smoothly, almost as if you have a fairy godmother or an unseen helper turning the wheels.

Alternatively, a real flesh-and-blood, human helper may turn up at the perfect moment to assist in some cherished venture. This colleague or companion could be someone new or someone you already know but never thought about in a partnership light before. Whoever they are, they'll be loyal, trustworthy, and their talents will complement your skills perfectly.

Together, the two of you will create something far better than either of you could have managed alone. If it's a business we're talking about, success is assured, but it looks like some Dogs will be embarking on a philanthropic project. Maybe you're launching a charity, setting up some sort of training school, providing shelter for the disadvantaged, or even opening a rescue centre for animals.

Whatever floats your boat, Dog. The important thing is that wherever you choose to deploy your energies this year, you'll be thrilled by the response. No longer will your efforts go unnoticed and unappreciated. Praise comes showering your way, and you may even earn yourself some sort of honour.

Money is not going to be a problem either this year, Dog. You're a metal creature and, as such, have an almost spooky knack of managing finances. Your new ventures will ensure cash starts rolling in, and even employed Dogs will be tempted to try a side hustle. There's never been a better time to go for it, Dog.

Relocating might not have been uppermost in the canine mind up to now, but 2026 could see some sort of issue regarding your home. Many Dogs could find unexpected circumstances cause them to consider a change of address. Don't be alarmed, this is not a resumption of bad luck. The zodiac Horse can see much further down the road than you can. A new place could be in your best interests and turn out to be unexpectedly delightful – a real blessing in disguise. So, if you need to move, don't grumble… seize the opportunity with enthusiasm.

Then there's that family of yours. The typical Dog can't be happy if their pack isn't happy. Dogs with relatives belonging to fire signs could find them even more hot-tempered than usual right now. Even the placid ones are likely to snap more easily. Yet if you manage to stay cool and referee the blazing rows in that clever way of yours, you may be able to bring lasting peace to a long-running quarrel. This could be the year the family comes together properly for the first time in decades.

One of the drawbacks of a fire year is the speed of events. You're a strong, energetic type, Dog, and you're capable of very rapid responses. Yet you don't like to be rushed. You want to choose when to activate your inner greyhound, not have the decision forced on you. Well, this year, even with the friendly influence of the Horse, you need to stay alert and be prepared to spring into action at a moment's notice. Fortunately, once the adrenaline kicks in, you'll find you rather enjoy life in the fast lane. What's more, the results of your quick thinking will prove hugely rewarding.

Then there's the uncanny way fire can start very small – as the tiniest spark – and then morph into a raging inferno in a trice. What you start this year, Dog, could grow into something huge – out of all proportion to the modest beginnings. Stay in control and you're in for one of the most exciting years of your life.

The Wonder of Being a Dog

You really are something special, Dog. Okay, if you're a typical hound, you're probably the modest type and scarcely even notice the qualities that single you out from other signs. Yet, in your own quiet way, you are admirable.

For some reason, there are cultures that don't respect dogs, but not China. The Chinese regard the zodiac sign of the Dog as a symbol of justice and compassion. Noble, honest, and fair, the true zodiac Dog is an incredibly valuable member of any society.

People born under this sign are the most loyal of friends, family members, and workmates. They will support their 'pack' to the bitter end, even if their own interests suffer as a consequence.

They attach great importance to fairness in every aspect of life, and for this reason, they're great believers in rules.

Even if they encounter a rule they don't like, they will follow it anyway – because they believe if everyone had a pick-and-choose attitude to which rules they obeyed, civilisation would collapse. The Dog is quite prepared to set a good example, even in the face of scorn from other signs.

Basically, the Dog is the most honest of all the signs. You can rely on Dog to do the right thing – always. Typical Dog is the one that hands back excess change when the shop assistant makes a mistake, notifies the bank if too much cash is credited to their account, and never fiddles a penny on any expenses they're allowed. For these reasons, other signs instinctively trust the Dog, even if they don't realise why.

Dogs make excellent workers, of course, and excel in management. As well as being intelligent, honest, and brave, their quest for fairness ensures they always give a fair day's work for whatever they're paid. Determined not to 'cheat' the boss, they usually end up doing far more than is necessary.

Yet employers are often baffled by their Dog staff. They mistake devotion and conscientiousness for driving ambition and can't understand, therefore, why the typical Dog seems uninterested in climbing the career ladder or competing for promotion. They assume Dog hasn't grasped the necessary methods when, in fact, the Dog is just more interested in what's going on at home.

Deep down, every Dog is longing to belong to a pack. Once they've found one and settled in, they're happy and content and – if necessary – will sacrifice themselves for the wellbeing of the others. And should a crisis occur, the typical Dog will be on the case instantly, probably leading the rescue party.

The Dog Home

The great thing about the Dog home is that it's a genuine home, not an interior design project. The typical Dog motto tends to be: 'You'll have to take me as you find me.'

They mean it too, so visitors need to be prepared for a lively melange of children, dogs, cats, and smaller pets of the moment, plus the detritus of various family hobbies and sports.

Furnishings are likely to be comfortable, well-worn, and scattered with pet hair, toys, and the occasional pet. Flooring sports muddy prints, paw or foot, the odd bowl of water, and more toys: dog, child, or both. The wallpaper may be starting to fade, but it hardly shows, covered as it is in kids' artwork and family photos.

Yet despite the slightly chaotic air, there's a happy atmosphere, and the Dog is a welcoming host. Guests are greeted warmly and pressed to stay for copious home-cooked snacks and huge mugs of whatever Dog is brewing. Visitors end up staying far longer than they intended and helping with the washing up, too.

Being Friends with the Dog

Anyone lucky enough to be friends with the Dog has a loyal mate for life. You can depend on Dog to be on your side, even when you're wrong. Dog will give you their last penny if you're in need and will turn up with soup, flowers, and something undemanding to read if you're sick. They'll feed your pets when you're away and pick up your children from school if you're delayed; it wouldn't even occur to them to ask for anything in return.

Moreover, the ever-responsible Dog has a surprisingly carefree side when relaxed. The Dog loves to play. Expect picnics and games and hours of silly fun when Dog's in the mood for some R&R.

The only problem with making such a delightful friend is that it takes a while for Dog to admit new faces to the charmed inner circle. Their friendly manner easily attracts new acquaintances, but they tend to remain acquaintances for quite a while. It takes time for Dog to bestow their trust, but when they do, it's unbreakable and unconditional.

The other thing to bear in mind is that Dog's honesty is unflinching. Never ask the Dog if a certain outfit makes you look fat, or a particular colour suits you, unless you really want to know the plain, unvarnished truth. Dog truly doesn't understand why you'd want anything less.

On the other hand, should Dog pay you a compliment, you know – without doubt – it's sincere.

Dog Superpowers
Bravery

Reliability

Competence

Best Jobs for Dog 2026
Aid Worker

Medical Professional

Detective

Teacher

Auditor

Kennel Manager

Perfect Partners

Cupid's arrow can strike anywhere at any time, of course, but once the novelty of new romance wears off, some relationships are easier to maintain than others. Here's a guide to the Dog compatibility with other signs.

Dog with Dog

Dogs love company so these two will gravitate to each other and stay there. Both are loyal, faithful types; neither need worry the other will stray. They'll appreciate their mutual respect for doing things properly and their shared love of a stable, caring home. This relationship is likely to last and last. The only slight hitch could occur if, over time, the romance dwindles and Dog and Dog become more like good friends than lovers.

Dog with Pig

In the outside world, the Dog and the Pig can get along well together; in fact, Pigs (being intelligent creatures) can do many of the things dogs can do, so it's not surprising this zodiac pair makes a good couple. Good-natured Pig is uncomplicated and fair-minded, which suits Dog perfectly. Also, Pig brings out Dog's playful side – which delights Pig, who's always keen to have a playmate. A happy relationship involving many restaurants.

Dog with Rat

The Rat and the Dog get along pretty well together. Both are strong characters who respect each other and give each other space when required. But deep down, the Dog is a worrier and gets anxious about unnecessary risks, while Rat just can't help sailing close to the wind if an interesting opportunity presents itself. Long-term, reckless Rat might unintentionally drive Dog to distraction. Only to be considered by Dogs with nerves of steel.

Dog with Ox

These two ought to get along well as they're both sensible, down-to-earth, loyal, hardworking, and in tune with each other's basic beliefs. And yet, somehow, they don't. Dog has a playful streak and finds this lacking in Ox, while Ox may be baffled by what seems like pointless silliness in Dog. If they can agree to differ, they could make a relationship work.

Dog with Tiger

While not exactly opposites, these two are different enough to intrigue each other yet similar enough in basic outlook to get on well. Both Tiger and Dog are idealistic and uninterested in material gain, yet where Dog can be nervous, Tiger is bold. And where Tiger attracts controversy, Dog will be loyal. This partnership could be lasting and valuable.

Dog with Rabbit

Despite the fact that in the outside world, Rabbit could easily end up as Dog's dinner, the astrological pair gets on surprisingly well. Dog appreciates Rabbit's careful, efficient ways and soft voice, while Rabbit admires Dog's energy and good intentions. Dog's lack of interest in the finer points of interior design might try Rabbit's patience, but with a little work, these two could reach an understanding.

Dog with Dragon

Not the easiest of combinations. Down-to-earth Dog can't see what all the fuss is about when it comes to Dragons. Unimpressed by glamour and irritated by what seems (to Dog) the gullibility of Dragon admirers, Dog can't be bothered to find out more. Dragon, meanwhile, is hurt by Dog's lack of interest. Great determination would be needed to make this work.

Dog with Snake

Some snakes seem to have an almost hypnotic power, and for some reason, Dog is particularly susceptible to these skills. We've heard of snake charmers, but snakes can be dog charmers, and without even trying, Snakes can find themselves the recipients of Dog devotion. Since the Dog is strong, loyal, and can be fun, Snake is not averse to this but might, in the end, find it boring.

Dog with Horse

Both are good friends of man; these two can make a formidable team. Dog understands the occasional need for solitude while admiring Horse's strength and agility. Horse, meanwhile, senses Dog's loyalty and down-to-earth nature. Both lovers of the great outdoors and physical activity, they'll never be short of adventures to share. A promising long-term relationship.

Dog with Goat

This is another relationship that could be tricky. Loyal Dog would be quite willing to stand by Goat when practical problems loom, but could end up irritated by Goat's inability to learn from previous mistakes, and so keeps making them. Goat can't understand why Dog gets so bothered. With care, these two could learn to live together.

Dog with Monkey

Monkey finds Dog intriguing. Monkey senses Dog's strength of character coupled with its playful streak, which fits well with Monkey's love of games. Dog, meanwhile, appreciates Monkey's energy and light-hearted approach. Yet before long, Monkey's disdain for rules will grate on Dog's instinctive love of them. They cannot agree in this area, and it could lead to arguments.

Dog with Rooster

Rooster and Dog are not the best of partners. Dog can be as plain-spoken as Rooster and is not likely to be impressed by overt behaviour. What's more, Dog is often critical, and Rooster can't stand criticism. Rooster, on the other hand, is likely to sense and resent Dog's attitude. Frustration abounds for both in this relationship. Only for the hopelessly love-struck.

Dog Love 2026 Style

Time to drag out your party threads, Dog! Kick off those wellies and do something creative with your hair. You're in demand this year, and you know you scrub up well if you put your mind to it.

Chances are, single Dogs are too preoccupied with an exciting new project to fuss too much with their appearance or romance. Yet the Horse is keen for you to partner up, Dog. You may not have realised it yet, but you're radiating sultry appeal right now. No need to laugh. You're temptation on legs this year. Thanks to the Horse, you're currently bathed in an irresistible glow that's turning heads wherever you go. Nothing you can do about it, Dog. Just step into the limelight and enjoy the attention.

Big gatherings will prove especially lucky for single Dogs. Admirers will gravitate to you despite the crush, and amongst them could be someone really special. Don't go stomping off like you often do because it's too crowded or you've got to get up early in the morning. Hang on in there, Dog. True love is looking for you, and this could be the year you find it.

Attached Dogs need to prioritise enthusing their partner with the great new canine project. This is especially important if it involves charity work or some sort of idealistic venture. Get them on board, and the two of you will be best friends as well as lovers. Fail to interest them and they might drift away, permanently.

Secrets of Success in 2026

You've never been the showy, boastful type about your talents, Dog. Yet in your quiet, understated way, you're usually successful at what you do. People tend to underestimate you, but that's often an advantage. Competitive rivals pay you little attention, then they're amazed when the prize unexpectedly drops into your lap rather than theirs. How exactly did you do that? Your miraculous good fortune nags at them for months afterwards. What secret could you possess that explains it?

Well, this year you're likely to be a little more up front about your plans. You're all fired up about an appealing idea and too eager to put it into practice to be secretive. The omens are good however you play it, but keep an eye open for a partner to help you hone the venture to perfection. Two heads will be even better than one this year, Dog.

Remember to think before you speak as much as possible. You can be famously 'frank' and pride yourself on stating the plain, unvarnished truth at all times. Honesty is the best policy after all, as far as Dog is concerned. But in this fire year, the more delicate signs are likely to take offence. You could lose much valuable support by failing to take the trouble to be tactful. A little honey goes a long way, Dog. Think sweetness and light, and you can't lose.

The Dog Year at a Glance

January – Sluggish vibes overtake the canine residence, and it's down to you to get them all moving. Is a nip to the ankles out of the question? Maybe a louder alarm clock…

February – Things are looking up at work. Leadership is required, and you are just the one to provide it.

March – Your pet project is beginning to take shape. A side hustle for now or should you commit full-time?

April – Romance turns a little rocky. A demanding person tries to take liberties. Can you agree, or should you say goodbye?

May – An unexpected letter arrives. At least it's not a bill. There could be complications, though. Think it over or get advice.

June – A possible partner appears on the scene. It could be a work colleague or a new acquaintance. Time to join forces?

July – A family member needs your expertise. You don't have much time to spare, but you can't say no. Do your best, Dog.

August – You love your big summer get-togethers. Round everyone up and prepare to party. If you don't have a garden, head for the park.

September – Your plans are well underway, but the resident busybody just has to criticise. Take no notice, Dog.

October – You're back on track. After a slight wobble last month, your plans are progressing nicely. Keep doing what you're doing.

November – Playful puppies tempt you away from the workplace. Aren't you too busy to lark about, Dog? Of course not!

December – Festivities at one of your wilder relatives' place. Will you wish you'd stayed at home? Nonsense, Dog. Relax, you'll have a ball.

Lucky colours for 2026: Tangerine, Ochre, Gold

Lucky numbers for 2026: 3, 8, 11

Three Takeaways

Choose your words carefully

Smile!

Play is the new work

CHAPTER 7: THE PIG

Pig Years

4 February 1935 – 23 January 1936
22 January 1947 – 9 February 1948
8 February 1959 – 27 January 1960
27 January 1971 – 14 February 1972
13 February 1983 – 1 February 1984
31 January 1995 – 18 February 1996
18 February 2007 – 6 February 2008
5 February 2019 – 24 January 2020
23 January 2031 – 10 February 2032
10 February 2043 – 29 January 2044
28 January 2055 – 14 February 2056

Natural Element: Water

Will 2026 be a Glorious Year for the Pig?

Now don't panic, Pig. Sit down for a moment and grab yourself a slice of something calming. The point is, you've just emerged from the year of the Snake and – to be honest – being under that cool serpent glare has made you a bit nervous all year. Hardly surprising, then, that you were hoping for a chance to relax and recharge in 2026.

Unfortunately, (or *maybe* in a strange way, fortunately for you), it doesn't look as if that hope will materialise. The vibrant Horse has come galloping in and looks likely to shake up the Pig residence all over again. This is particularly unsettling as the delightful Pig has little experience of less than sympathetic rulers.

The inoffensive Pig has the good fortune to be favoured by nearly all the zodiac signs. Cheerful, well-meaning, and no threat to anyone, the majority of even the grumpiest of signs can find time for the cute little dude with the trotters. As a result, it's often nearly a decade at a time before the Pig encounters any friction. So now, many Pigs are experiencing something of a double whammy. First, in 2025, came the unsympathetic Snake. Snake doesn't dislike the Pig particularly, but just can't see the point of many Piggy enthusiasms, so is not inclined to support them.

And now, here's the boisterous Horse. The Horse is quite prepared to befriend another farmyard cousin. Trouble is, from the Pig's point of view, Horse is rather large and overwhelming, and given to racing about far too much. The pace of a Horse year is uncomfortably fast, as far as most Pigs are concerned.

So, for the second year in a row, the typical Pig is being urged to get up out of their comfort zone and do things a little differently.

This is probably not welcome news to many Pigs because you like your comfort and you've got your favoured zone just the way you want it. Yet the Horse won't stand for such a sedentary attitude. The Horse wants you off the sofa and out there exploring the wider world. And you know what, Pig? When you actually take the plunge, you're going to love it.

Travel is in the stars for many Pigs this year. And we're not talking a quick visit to that elderly relative an hour or two away. Long-distance adventures have got your name on them, even if the thought of holidays hasn't even crossed your mind yet. Unexpected events will conspire in such a way that, before long, many a Pig will be browsing the airline schedules and checking out hotels. Or maybe it's an exotic cruise to distant shores that suddenly turns up.

Some lucky Pigs won't even have to splash out on their foreign travels. The trip could be gifted to you for a special occasion, or maybe you're the winner of a fabulous competition. Either way, Pig, chances are your new globe-trotting is going to cost much less than you think.

Then there's the Pig career. Although many Pigs aren't overtly ambitious, they're actually excellent operators when they can be bothered to engage with the hectic world of work. Pigs make very good managers, too. Their affable manner ensures they're popular with all the staff, and their gentle words put everyone at ease. People are often surprised at how diligent Pig can turn out to be, because that happy-go-lucky personality can suggest a careless approach. Yet once the Pig fully commits to a task, their dedication is total.

This year, Pig, if you're typical of your sign, you may find you're either propelled into a new job that you never intended to attempt, or you get some sort of promotion or relocation forced upon you. No good sighing, Pig. These changes are actually wonderful opportunities. Once you get stuck in, you'll manage your new roles with ease, and the rewards will be better than you could ever have dreamed.

Business Pigs, on the other hand, could be talked into diversifying in 2026. It's sensible to be cautious, of course, but don't dismiss new ideas just because you've not tackled that sort of thing before. A radical update could be just the boost your venture needs.

Then there's money. If you're typical of your sign, Pig, you have a bit of a complicated relationship with cash. Plenty seems to come in, but even more seems to flow out. You do like to spend, and temptation surrounds you wherever you go.

This year, once again, wealth is pouring into the Pig coffers, but there are likely to be even more demands on your cash. This is because the fire energy of the year is bringing you exciting opportunities everywhere you look, yet because you're a water creature, fire fears to come too close.

So instead of building up, your wealth tends to falter and get nibbled away by excess spending and unexpected bills. But don't despair, Pig. Find an accountant or team up with a sensible sign with a knack for finance, and hand your money matters over to them. You never know. By this time next year, you could be a millionaire!

The Wonder of Being a Pig

There are so many wonderful things about you, Pig, it's difficult to know where to start.

Yet, in the West, the Pig is often regarded at best as a figure of fun, and at worst as an insult. Jokes around over-eating, messy homes, or grubby habits abound; the zodiac Pig has to develop a good sense of humour to cope.

Fortunately, this isn't difficult as the typical Pig is the most amiable of personalities. Pig is quite prepared to laugh along with everyone else and rarely takes teasing personally.

Attitudes are quite different in the East. The Chinese regard the Pig as a lucky sign, symbolic of abundance and prosperity. Maybe it's something to do with the healthy Pig's lavish amount of flesh or its miraculous fertility that can produce 14 little piglets in one litter. No family, it is believed, can be poor if it's fortunate enough to own a pig.

Zodiac Pigs are neither aggressive nor competitive, so they have no enemies among the other celestial animals. They get on with almost everyone. In fact, few people actually dislike the Pig – the worst the pig ever endures is indifference. Or possibly mild irritation.

People born under this sign are naturally happy. They're tolerant and easy going and see the best in everyone. They're also generous and sympathetic, so they tend to be suckers for hard luck stories. What's more, they'll be taken in again and again by the same person because they believe everyone should be given the benefit of a second chance.

The Pig is only human, of course, and can occasionally be roused to anger but such outbursts are rare.

The most important thing to the Pig – absolutely central to Pig's philosophy – is that life is about having a good time. The Pig just wants to be happy and desires everyone else to be happy, too.

What's more, the Pig finds happiness in the simplest of things. You don't need to spend a fortune to cheer the Pig up or lay on a host of adrenalin-boosting pursuits. The Pig is delighted by cream cakes, freshly baked bread, and chocolate galore – in fact, tasty food of any kind.

Pigs love to laugh, go out dancing, or just lie in the sun.

This is an immensely sensuous sign. Velvet and cashmere, the feeling of grass beneath bare feet, or the scent of spring flowers – these are the things that make the Pig's day.

You're unlikely to find the Pig slogging around a marathon course or taking up rock climbing. Strenuous sports are not the typical Pig's thing. Shopping, however, is a different matter. The Pig is a champion shopper. If shopping was an Olympic sport, Pig would win gold every time.

It's not that Pig is greedy; it just can't resist pretty things and tends to find them on every expedition. Which is where other signs sometimes get irritated with the Pig. The Pig is notoriously bad with money and can't help overspending. Discipline is not a strong point when it comes to cash and food.

Fortunately, most Pigs are highly intelligent, do well at work, and are not normally short of cash. It's just the more they earn, the more lovely things they think they can buy.

The Pig Home

Pig has heard the expression 'less is more' but doesn't quite get it. What is the point of having less of the things you like, Pig wonders, when you could have more? Who would willingly do such a thing?

Should you find Pig in a minimalist home, chances are it belongs to someone else and Pig can't wait to move.

The real Pig home tends to be comfortable and warm and overflowing with 'objects'. Pig does a lot of shopping and the resulting treasures have to be proudly displayed throughout Pig's quarters. Many Pigs are great collectors, too, anything from Royal Doulton China to Art Deco bronzes, from ancient stamp collections to vintage clothes. The Pig delights in tracking down the perfect pieces, and one is not enough.

Inside the Pig palace, you're spoiled for novelty scatter cushions and jungles of pot plants, while the kitchen is so well equipped with every conceivable gadget it would make MasterChef envious.

Most true Pigs are excellent cooks and they believe in quality *plus* quantity when it comes to meals. Visitors lucky enough to be invited to dinner are guaranteed a memorable feast.

Being Friends with the Pig

The typical Pig has a great many friends, and it's not difficult to see why. The Pig enjoys company, is an uncritical companion, and is quite happy to fall in with whatever the others want to do as long as it's not too strenuous.

What's more, the Pig is always on the lookout for innocent fun, and has a knack for turning the most unpromising situation into a jolly adventure. You'll invariably end up enjoying yourself on jaunts with the Pig.

In fact, the only downside to having a piggy friend is that you're likely to put on weight – any time is the perfect time for coffee and cakes or a cheeky G&T as far as Pig's concerned – or you'll end up broke from all those shopping expeditions.

It takes a great deal of discipline to be friends with the Pig, but most mates reckon it's worth it.

Pig Superpowers

A sunny nature

Kind heart

Unlimited capacity for fun

Best Jobs for Pig 2026

Pastry Chef

Party Planner

Vet

Dancer

Hairdresser

Perfect Partners

Cupid's arrow can strike anywhere at any time, of course, but once the novelty of new romance wears off, some relationships are easier to maintain than others. Here's a guide to the Pig's compatibility with other signs.

Pig with Pig

When one Pig sets eyes on another Pig, they can't help moving closer for a better look, and should they get talking they probably won't stop. These two understand each other and share so many interests and points of view they seem like a perfect couple. Yet, long-term, they can end up feeling too alike. Pigs rarely argue, yet oddly enough, they can find themselves squabbling over trivialities with another Pig. Care needed.

Pig with Rat

It's very easy for Rat to be beguiled by the Pig. Pig's easy-going, sympathetic nature immediately relaxes the Rat. What's more, Pig loves shopping as much as Rat so the two of them could enjoy many happy expeditions together. Conflict could occur through overspending. Pig does not understand Rat's compulsion to bag a bargain. Pig will buy whatever the price and the two could end up arguing over money.

Pig with Ox

Delightful Pig will catch Ox's eye, and since Pig isn't a constant thrill-seeker, the two of them could enjoy many peaceful evenings together, perhaps over a tasty meal. Yet Pig's spendthrift ways – at least in Ox's eyes – could soon prove very annoying as well as illogical to the Ox, while Pig could find Ox's attitude judgmental and upsetting. Not ideal for the long term.

Pig with Tiger

Carefree Pig will love to bask in Tiger's impressive aura, while Tiger will feel good about protecting this charming but unworldly creature. They enjoy each other's company and Tiger, so focused on lofty matters, will find Pig's compulsive shopping too trivial to worry about. This couple could do well together as long as Pig's fondness for cosy nights in doesn't make Tiger feel trapped.

Pig with Rabbit

Pig is not quite as interested in fine dining as Rabbit, and is happy to scoff a burger as much as a cordon bleu creation, but their shared love of the good things in life makes these two happy companions. Once again, Pig's spending habits might irritate Rabbit, but not too much, as Rabbit is quite willing to splurge on lovely things for the home. A relationship would work well.

Pig with Dragon

While Dragon and Pig might seem to be opposites, the two of them can create a surprisingly contented relationship. Pig is quite happy for Dragon to fly around doing exciting things as long as Pig is not expected to do much more than admire profusely. Dragon appreciates Pig's uncritical support and makes allowances for Pig's lack of stamina. This couple could live in harmony.

Pig with Snake

Pig and Snake don't have a lot to say to each other. Snake can't be bothered with Pig's endless shopping, and Pig is hurt by Snake's snobbish attitude. They both enjoy the good things in life, so a luxury fling could briefly be fun – a shared spa break might be a good idea – but in the long term, this relationship is probably not worth pursuing.

Pig with Horse

Pig and Horse are good companions. Horse is soothed by easy-going Pig, and Pig is proud to be seen with such an alluring creature as Horse. They don't have a lot of interests in common, but they don't antagonise each other either. They can jog along amicably for quite a while, but in the long term, they may find they each want more than the other can provide.

Pig with Goat

Happy-go-lucky Pig and laid-back Goat make a good pair. They hate to stir up trouble and always look for a peaceful solution to any challenge. Ideally, they'd avoid the challenge altogether. They could be very contented together as long as Pig's spending and Goat's inability to deal with finances doesn't get them into trouble.

Pig with Monkey

On the surface, these two might seem an unlikely couple. Yet Pig enjoys Monkey's fun and humour while Monkey is happy to be admired uncritically. What's more, Monkey's inventive mind can solve any difficulties caused by Pig's spending, and since Monkey can't resist a challenge, the opportunity to retrain Pig or at least find a way to obtain purchases cheaper could help the relationship last.

Pig with Rooster

These two might seem an unlikely couple – modest Pig with extrovert Rooster. Yet Pig has no need or wish to crow, and can see the vulnerable character that lurks beneath Rooster's fine feathers. While Rooster responds to Pig's kindness and undemanding nature. As long as Rooster doesn't get bored, this can be a contented relationship.

Pig with Dog

In the outside world, the dog and the pig can get along well together; in fact, pigs, being intelligent creatures, can do many of the things dogs can do, so it's not surprising this zodiac pair make a good couple. Good-natured Pig is uncomplicated and fair-minded, which suits Dog perfectly. Also, Pig brings out Dog's playful side – which delights Pig, who's always keen to have a playmate. A happy relationship involving many restaurants.

Pig Love 2026 Style

Well, Pig, you've always been a seductive sign, but this year you excel yourself. When the massive fire energy of 2026 collides with the water vibe of Ms or Mr Pig, the result is bound to be an explosion of steam. So yes, things will get decidedly steamy in the Pig boudoir right now.

Let's face it, you're a very sexy sign, Pig. You always were. In anyone else, your irresistible charms would arouse jealousy from less enticing rivals. Yet you exude such innocent joy and such an infectious sense of fun that even the most green-eyed competitors are won over. You don't mean to snatch all the attention, they understand, you just want everyone to enjoy themselves. It's not your fault if some signs get the wrong idea.

Passions are running very high this year, though Pig, particularly amongst the fire signs, so don't get too naughty, especially with a flamey type, unless you really mean it. Broad-minded Pig sees no harm in a little flirty fun, but not all your admirers share your relaxed attitude. Be careful what you agree to, Pig, or you could end up in over your head.

Attached Pigs are set for a roller coaster year with their beloved. You hate to quarrel, but the fiery atmosphere is likely to affect your partner. Storms and misunderstandings could reverberate around the Pig palace for no reason at all. Yet you are a peace maker extraordinaire, Pig. Making up will be sensational.

Secrets of Success in 2026

You seldom lose much sleep worrying about success, Pig. Life's too short to agonise, as far as you're concerned. Yet success invariably finds you anyway, simply because you're so comfortable to be around. Just by being your natural self, things usually work out fine.

Yet, this year, you really could achieve something special if you remember a couple of basic tips. First, many unusual and previously untried opportunities are likely to come your way in the next few months. Don't be reckless, but try to say 'yes' to as many as possible, even if they don't sound like your normal 'thing'. That's the *whole point*, Pig. The Horse is attempting to give you a completely new perspective; the chance to broaden your horizons. This can only be beneficial, Pig, so don't resist.

Second, be sure to pace yourself and stay calm. Take up yoga or meditation or something similarly soothing. The energy this year is strong, rapid, and demanding, and it can easily exhaust sensitive signs such as yourself, Pig. You certainly have all the ability you need to cope, but in order to activate it, you must be tranquil. Take your time, don't panic, and quietly think things through before making a decision. Just stick to these simple rules and you'll be cracking open the champagne before the year's out.

The Pig Year at a Glance

January – You can't work out why some people don't like January. If they keep the party going all month like you do, Pig, it's fun, fun, fun. Plus, of course, you've got the sales. Pure joy.

February – An older person wants to take you under their wing. You can manage quite well as it is, but it would be rude to refuse.

March – You and your besties are planning a trip or three. Seaside special, anyone?

April – The boss has a surprise for you. New premises? New responsibilities? New colleagues? All good, Pig.

May – A younger person wants your advice. Could be something technical. If you're not sure, don't improvise. Ask an expert.

June – A close friend or relative has a wonderful gift for you. You're feeling quite emotional.

July – You love to entertain, and the gang is coming over. Menu planning, food shopping, a ton of cooking to do. You're in your element, Pig.

August – It went so well last month, you're organising another feast. Out of doors this time. You're so good at this, you could turn professional, Pig.

September – A long-distance trip beckons. Dust off the passport and dig out those suitcases. You're going to need a lot of gear.

October – An old flame returns and misunderstandings get complicated. You'll need a good excuse.

November – Almost Christmas – your fave time of year. The shops, the lights, the carols – it's almost better than the big day itself…

December – …but not quite! Looks like you might have to hire a van to carry all your gifts to the party this year. Pig Heaven.

Lucky colours for 2026: Silver, Tan, Amber

Lucky numbers for 2026: 1, 2, 9

Three Takeaways

Employ an accountant
Keep calm
Try something new

CHAPTER 8: THE RAT

Rat Years

5 February 1924 – 24 January 1925
24 January 1936 – 10 February 1937
10 February 1948 – 28 January 1949
28 January 1960 – 14 February 1961
15 February 1972 – 2 February 1973
2 February 1984 – 19 February 1985
19 February 1996 – 7 February 1997
7 February 2008 – 25 January 2009
25 January 2020 – 11 February 2021
11 February 2032 – 30 January 2033
30 January 2044 – 16 February 2045

Natural Element: Water

Will 2026 be a Glorious Year for the Rat?

Buckle up, Rat. You never could resist a challenge, so this year should be truly invigorating. Sharpen up those razor wits, practise some of your speciality, lightning turns, and prepare to grab the speeding Horse. Leap aboard and learn to ride.

Yes, you're quite right if you have sussed that 2026 will be a little more complicated than the past two years, Rat. Back then, we had the Dragon of 2024, which adored you, followed by the slightly less amiable Snake of 2025. The Snake, though shrewd and more sceptical of your rodent ways, was still prepared to assist in your most cherished schemes. As a result, even though you may not have ended up living in paradise surrounded by every luxury a Rat could desire, you must admit (if you're typical of your sign), you haven't got too much to complain about. You've done pretty well for yourself.

So now it's only fair if some of the other signs get first turn at the choicest favours, isn't it, Rat? This doesn't mean the Horse dislikes you, just that – as you're not a special friend – you'll have to work a bit harder to attract equine luck.

Oddly enough, this won't faze the typical Rat at all. In fact, secretly, many a rodent will relish the prospect. The game is almost more rewarding than the prize as far as Rats are concerned. And if it's too easy, it spoils the fun. Super-intelligent Rat delights in the opportunity to crack a code, solve a problem, or outwit a rival. Bring it on, the *more difficult the better* is Rat's attitude.

It's not as if you'll be short of opportunities this year, Rat. You and the Horse both love speed and action, and you share a surprising amount of stamina. You have a lot in common when you think about it, despite the difference in stature. What's more, the sudden and unexpected changes of direction to which the Horse is prone don't bother you either. Wily Rat has whirlwind reflexes and can reroute in a trice if necessary.

In many ways, you're ideally suited to a Horse year, Rat. The only drawback is that the Horse is a fire creature, and you belong to the water element. So the two of you are never going to be at ease with each other. Deep down, you sense that each could destroy the other if they really went for it. No wonder you're both wary and don't like to get too close. In everyday life, this hesitancy could play out as a series of irritating delays or unexpected obstacles blocking your path.

Rats are born entrepreneurs, even those employed in other jobs, and in 2026, you could spot a very promising new venture. You just know – in your bones – this is a brilliant idea that can't fail. Yet setting it up is likely to prove far more difficult than you expected. If you hang on in there, Rat, you're likely to succeed in the end, but *prepare for frustration*.

Employed Rats always do well at work, and this year is no exception. Yet some Rats could find themselves landed with an unwelcome set of new rules that slow you down and force you to reorganise for no sensible reason. Other Rats may have to deal with a new authority figure who wants to question everything they do or interfere with their routines.

Devise a clever plan to circumnavigate the whole inefficient lot, Rat, and you could end up running the company before the year's out!

Many Rats could find themselves overseeing major projects on the home front in 2026. You're not normally a particularly fussy type, but right now a certain restlessness around your living quarters has developed. You can see all sorts of ways to enlarge, redesign, maybe even knock everything down and start again if you can get permission. It might be simpler to move, Rat, but once you get started, you're keen to see it through. Once again, unexpected hitches are likely to cause delays and extra expense, but stick with it. It'll be lovely when it's finished!

You have a wonderful knack with people, Rat, but this year the faces around you could prove demanding and delightful in equal measure. On the demanding side, the fire element could turn a family member awkward and bad-tempered. You'll need all your formidable management skills to tame their tantrums. On the delightful side, the lively atmosphere will draw new friends to your side. Many a Rat will be joining forces with like-minded individuals to create some sort of organisation – either social or business or maybe a mix of both. Either way, this group will bring you lasting satisfaction. You might even end up with a national following. This could be the start of something big, Rat.

Expect fiery squabbles around your beloved Rat pack, too, but don't worry unnecessarily. There's no cause for alarm. They'll sort themselves out, and it might be best to leave them to it and refuse to get involved.

And finally, though many Rats are not especially interested in long-distance travel, there'll be even more scurrying around than usual this year. Your journeys may not be long, but there will be plenty of them, and you could travel to a place you've never visited before. When you find it, this place charms you so much that you return over and over again. Maybe you've found your paradise after all, Rat. Enjoy!

The Wonder of Being a Rat

Have you got over it yet, Rat? Discovering the name of your zodiac sign, that is? Not exactly a compliment, you might think. You're not exactly going to boast about being a Rat to your friends, are you?

The flesh and blood creature must be one of the most despised beasts on the planet. No community, probably anywhere in the world, wants a rat on its doorstep. Drastic steps – no matter how horrible – are regarded as necessary by even the gentlest of people to eradicate rats altogether.

Well, clear your mind of all that bad press, Rat, because the zodiac Rat is a different proposition altogether.

The Chinese recognise that while they might not welcome a colony of rats to set up in their homes, the essential energy that animates the Rat is highly admirable.

For a start, the fact that constant efforts to eradicate rodents by humans worldwide always fail demonstrates the Rat's amazing survival skills. The species is immensely successful. Quick, intelligent, and tenacious, they'd be praised for these wonderful qualities if they were human beings.

So, far from being an unfortunate sign, being born in the year of the Rat is regarded as a good omen.

You should have inherited all the positive characteristics of your little furry namesake, Rat, if you're typical of your sign, plus charm, elegance, and good taste.

Few Rats are shy, and they are also gregarious, so they have no difficulty popping into a roomful of strangers and instantly striking up a conversation. In fact, the typical Rat relishes just such a challenge.

Mental stimulation of almost any kind is essential for the lively Rat, along with chalking up a victory, since Rat is also the competitive type. For this reason, Rats love shopping and hunting for bargains. The typical Rat seldom pays full price for anything and savours the triumph of the deal probably more than the cut-price item they've just acquired.

Natural entrepreneurs and adventurers, Rats are always on the lookout for business ideas, commercial alliances, and more deals. They never stop. 'The Rat Race' is all a bit of a game to the Rat. In fact, Rat is quite happy to take a risk and finds the element of danger exciting. 'You've got to speculate to accumulate' is one of Rat's favourite sayings, and Rat does a lot of speculating.

Unfortunately, this tendency leads many a Rat into gambling and/or get-rich-quick schemes – often unwisely. Rats can lose money this way, yet they'll do it all again next time around as the thrill is irresistible. And being the great survivors they are, Rats have an uncanny knack for scuttling out of trouble when the going gets tough. They seldom suffer the worst consequences of their disasters.

Above all, family is of immense importance to the typical Rat. While they have a wide circle of friends, family comes first, always. Beneath that easy bonhomie, Rats are shrewd and ambitious – they sail to the top, but – at the end of the day – the rewards are all for their family. If your breadwinner happens to be a Rat, you'll never go hungry.

The Rat Home

Invitations to the Rat home tend to be given out quite regularly. Rat regards home as an ideal place to network and strike deals, as well as the perfect background for stimulating get-togethers and family events.

Rat also has innate good taste and enjoys shopping, so the rodent abode is likely to be fashionable, equipped with the latest technology – acquired at a bargain price – and faintly reminiscent of an upmarket hotel. In fact, the furnishings may well have been bought wholesale from some hospitality supplier.

Between visitors, the Rat home is probably found to be messy and draped with various members of the Rat extended clan: devouring snacks and gaming on Rat's 219-inch TV screen. Rat doesn't mind, though, because the typical rodent is out most of the time, pursuing important Rat business. As long as they muck in and restore order before clients are due, Rat is happy.

Being Friends with the Rat

As long as you're prepared to be one of many, it's easy being friends with the Rat. Rat enjoys mixing business with pleasure, so if you have some professional link or a network that might be useful to Rat, you're likely to be welcomed with particular warmth. Rat is renowned for inviting armies of workmates to the Rat wedding or christening of a rodent child.

A business connection is not essential, though. Rat enjoys company; the more, the merrier. As a Rat friend, you will enjoy generous hospitality, witty conversation, and uproarious evenings out.

The only downside is that the Rat is usually so busy, and get-togethers are frequently postponed. In Rat's world, family and business come first. As long as you can accept second place, it's great to be friends with the Rat.

Rat Superpowers

Quick wit

Shrewd eye for a bargain

Never lost for words

Best Jobs for Rat in 2026

Politician

Business Owner

Market Stallholder

Any form of sales

Public Relations

Advertising

Perfect Partners 2026

Cupid's arrow can strike anywhere at any time, of course, but once the novelty of new romance wears off, some relationships are easier to maintain than others. Here's a guide to the Rat's compatibility with other signs.

Rat with Rat

These two are certainly on the same wavelength and share many interests. When their eyes first meet, passionate sparks may fly. This relationship could work very well although, over time, the competitive and ambitious nature of both partners could see them pulling in different directions. What's more, if one should succumb to a weakness for gambling or risky business ventures while the other does not, it will end in tears.

Rat with Ox

Oddly enough, this combination can be surprisingly successful. Frenetic Rat and calm Ox may seem to be opposites but, in fact, Rat can find Ox's laid-back approach strangely soothing. Ox is not interested in competing with Rat and will put up with Rat's scurrying after new schemes with patience. As long as Rat doesn't get bored and has enough excitement in other areas of life, this relationship could be very contented.

Rat with Tiger

The magnificent Tiger will always catch Rat's eye because Rat loves beautiful things, but Tiger's natural element is Wood and Rat's is Water which means that Tiger wears Rat out. What's more, Tiger's not interested in Rat's latest bargain, and Rat doesn't share Tiger's passion for changing the world, yet the attraction is strong. If Rat makes an effort to step back and not get in Tiger's way, they could reach a good understanding.

Rat with Rabbit

Rat finds Rabbit intriguing. Here is an attractive, stylish creature that doesn't feel the need to be pushy or take centre stage yet somehow manages to be at the heart of things. The Rat wants to find out more, while Rabbit is flattered and entertained by witty Rat's attention. These two respect each other, but over the long term, Rat could be too overpowering.

Rat with Dragon

This couple is usually regarded as a very good match. They have much in common, being action-loving, excitement-seeking personalities who hate to be bored. It takes a lot to dazzle Rat, but the Dragon's glamorous aura proves irresistible, while Dragon loves to be admired, so each enjoys being with the other. There could be the odd power struggle as these two are both strong characters, but the magnetism is so powerful they usually kiss and make up.

Rat with Snake

The Snake shares Rat's good taste, and being elegant, sophisticated, and smart will delight Rat at first sight. These two get on very well on an intellectual level but perhaps are better as good friends rather than long-term partners. The Snake's love of basking in the sun for hours strikes Rat as lazy and dull, while Rat's need to rush around doing deals and meeting people seems pointless and wearying to the Snake.

Rat with Horse

Rat and Horse both fizz with energy and they love action and looking good, yet this is not seen as an ideal partnership. Nothing's impossible, of course, but these two will have to work hard to find harmony. The Rat will admire Horse's enthusiasm and cheerful approach but become impatient to discover Horse can also be fiery and emotional. Horse, on the other hand, can find Rat's risk-taking behaviour extremely worrying.

Rat with Goat

The Rat is charmed by carefree Goat and fascinated by its artistic talent and happy knack of living in the present. Easy-going Goat tends to like everyone, so is perfectly content to enjoy Rat's company. These two can get along fine, yet they don't really understand each other deep down. Long-term, the Rat may find Goat's lack of interest in the practical side of life, such as finances and bills, irritating.

Rat with Monkey

Unlikely as it might appear, mischievous Monkey and the clever Rat make a good partnership. Their quick minds, sociable natures, and love of novelty ensure that they're never bored together. True, Rat might sometimes feel Monkey is too inclined to skim over the surface of things and could do with being more serious at times, but Monkey's ingenuity and audaciousness always save the day. Both can have a weakness for gambling, though, so need to take care.

Rat with Rooster

The first thing Rat notices about the Rooster is its beautiful plumage, but this a relationship which is unlikely to get much further than initial admiration. Rooster's direct and frank approach can strike the Rat as tactless, while the Rooster can't understand why Rat has to make life so convoluted and complicated. Then again, Rooster's natural confidence and aplomb can come across as bragging to the Rat. These two have to be very determined to make a partnership work.

Rat with Dog

The Rat and the Dog get along pretty well together. Both are strong characters, and they respect each other and give each other space when required. But deep down, the Dog is a worrier and gets anxious about unnecessary risks, while Rat just can't help sailing close to the wind if an interesting opportunity presents itself. Long-term, reckless Rat might unintentionally drive Dog to distraction. Only to be considered by Dogs with nerves of steel.

Rat with Pig

It's very easy for Rat to be beguiled by the Pig. Pig's easy-going, sympathetic nature immediately relaxes the Rat. What's more, Pig loves shopping as much as Rat so the two of them could enjoy many happy expeditions together. Conflict could occur through overspending. Pig does not understand Rat's compulsion to bag a bargain, while Rat can't fathom why Pig is prepared to pay whatever's asked. However, with compromise on both sides, this could work well.

Rat Love 2026 Style

You just can't fail, Rat. You've never had problems finding a date. If you fell into a patch of mud and emerged wet, mucky, and with clumps of clay hanging from your hair (highly unlikely, you're the most agile of signs), your irresistible charms are so magnetic that other signs would be fighting over each other to pick you up, dust you down, and take you out for a restorative meal.

You can't help it, Rat. You've got a sparkling personality that dazzles and delights. It's effortless for you, and besotted admirers just can't get enough of your company. Sadly, for them, the typical single Rat has a 'more the merrier' attitude that extends to partners. You tend to skim lightly through a succession of relationships and can't see why anyone should object. What's the harm if everyone's having fun, the single Rat thinks. You like to move on frequently but have a happy knack of staying friends with former conquests, often for years.

Settling down is such a serious business that many Rats postpone making a decision until later in life. Family, friends, and business are

Rat's top priorities, and selecting a forever partner to fit in isn't easy. Yet 2026 could just bring the change you need. The right person could be waiting on the edge of the crowd. Slow down, Rat, and take *another* look.

Attached Rats could experience a roller-coaster year with their beloved, especially if beloved happens to belong to a fire sign. Your other half is likely to be extra moody, argumentative, or stubborn for no reason that makes sense to you. Be patient, Rat, and just blame the Horse. On the plus side, when they're up, they're really up, and you can do no wrong.

Secrets of Success in 2026

You may not realise it, Rat, but you're already a success. Almost everything you set out to do, you achieve. Should you ever find you're lacking funds, it's probably because you've gambled them on some risky venture, or invested in a get-rich-quick scheme which you knew deep down was probably a scam (but which you did anyway for the sheer thrill of seeing what would happen).

What's more, when the cash runs out, it doesn't take long for you to accumulate more. Your quick brain spots new opportunities in an instant, you're the master of lateral thinking, and with your silver tongue you can persuade almost anyone to agree to anything.

With all that going for you, you're confident you can cope with whatever this year might throw at you and still come up waving a fistful of banknotes.

Well, yes, you're right, Rat. But thanks to the Horse, you could do more than just hang onto your cash. You could really make it big in 2026 if you just play things a little differently. When the Horse is in charge, events move swiftly, and when the fire element is added on top they rocket through faster still. As a quick-moving Rat, this is fun for you. You enjoy speed. It doesn't scare you. The typical rodent finds racing about to be exhilarating.

So, it may not be welcome news, but this is the moment to do the opposite. To break the habit of a lifetime and *slow things down*. Try to keep up with the bolting Horse and you're likely to career out of control. The pace is too much even for your phenomenal grip.

Instead, insist on a little more time when it comes to business and career matters. Refuse to make decisions instantly, even though you can. Double-check all the figures and maybe discuss your ideas with some laid-back friends. This won't be easy for you to do. You can be the impatient type, Rat. But force the Horse to revert to walking pace through Rat territory and you can help yourself to all the good fortune you fancy.

The Rat Year at a Glance

January – Oops. Somehow, the Rat home looks like an army has trampled through. All that partying has its downside. Housework's not your thing, Rat. Recruit a bunch of friends.

February – a new boss is keen to meet all the staff. Colleagues seem nervous. Rat charm to the rescue.

March – Interior décor is suddenly on everyone's mind. They're sprucing things up in the workplace, and improvements are required at Rat Towers. You hate the smell of paint. Go out, Rat.

April – The new boss, or maybe the top dog, has spotted your genius, Rat. There's a deal to be done while they're in a good mood.

May – The work at Rat Towers has revealed more in-depth exploration is required. Time to get seriously involved in new plans.

June – Parties and weddings galore. You're too busy to be honest, but you can't miss the chance to network.

July – A new acquaintance has a brilliant idea and would like you to come on board. It could be the chance of a lifetime. Are they legit? Check them out, Rat.

August – It seems like the new face is all they appear to be. This could be the start of a beautiful partnership.

September – Your social life is getting complicated. A date gets the wrong idea, just as you want to say goodbye.

October – A family member disapproves. Is it any of their business? Probably not Rat, but try to keep the peace.

November – Bills, bills, and more bills. No, this is not the time to order another credit card.

December – The alterations are nowhere near finished, but it looks like everyone's back to Rat Towers again for the festivities. No one cares about the mess, and neither do you.

Lucky colours for 2026: Black, Silver, Red

Lucky numbers for 2026: 3, 5, 6

Three Takeaways
Think, patience
No need to run
Make time for family

CHAPTER 9: THE OX

Ox Years

25 January 1925 – 12 February 1926

11 February 1937 – 30 January 1938

29 January 1949 – 16 February 1950

15 February 1961 – 4 February 1962

3 February 1973 – 22 January 1974

20 February 1985 – 8 February 1986

8 February 1997 – 27 January 1998

26 January 2009 – 13 February 2010

12 February 2021 – 31 January 2022

31 January 2033 – 18 February 2034

17 February 2045 – 5 February 2046

4 February 2057 – 23 January 2058

Natural Element: Water

Will 2026 be a Glorious year for the Ox?

So, what do you think of it so far, Ox? The Snake of 2025 was good to most Oxen, and you've come through the year feeling pretty good if you're typical of your sign. Still got that wary feeling, though? That's just your highly developed survival instinct, ever on the alert. Relax Ox. 2026 is going to be just fine.

Admittedly, you may not have such an easy ride as you did last year. The Snake of 2025 was particularly fond of you and smoothed your path wherever possible. As a result, the typical Ox was able to enjoy a little more R&R than usual and probably benefited from some extra helpers, too.

The result is you start the new year in good shape, primed and ready to take advantage of some wonderful opportunities on offer from the Crimson Horse.

Okay, so you might be sceptical. The reason, though most Oxen probably won't realise it, is that deep down you sense you and the Horse are ancient rivals. You're both valuable farm creatures, both big and strong. You can both pull a plough or transport heavy items, yet you're not interchangeable. You have different strengths and weaknesses. Where the Horse is fast, you are slow. Where the Horse is showy and loves dressing up, you hate wasting time on pointless fripperies. Plus, the Horse can be moody and unpredictable, while you're always steady and ready to work. So, if only one of you is required for the job, which one should the farmer choose? While it's obvious who you would go for, Ox, you've often lost out to the annoyingly speedy Horse over the years.

So it's understandable if you're not exactly thrilled to hear your old competitor is in charge this year. Yet 2026 could be the making of you, Ox. The Horse is bringing you the chance to absorb the equine advantages that have allowed Horse to become so successful. Imagine how formidable the combination of your two talents would be. Your strength, stamina, and reliability, blended with Horse's agility and va-va voom. You'd be unstoppable, Ox.

The pace of this year, then, is going to be fast. You don't like that, Ox. New job offers, an expansion of Ox's business plans, the necessity for sudden trips, family and friends organising frequent holidays – all come pelting at you in dizzying succession.

If you're typical of your sign, Ox, you're likely to resist – purely because you object to the sheer scale and speed of the changes suggested. You need time to think, to ponder, to work out the pros and cons. Well, there's no time for that in 2026. This is a fire year, and fire doesn't do slow. Many Oxen will simply be forced to make decisions quickly. As excruciatingly uncomfortable as this seems, once the new regime comes into play, you'll be surprised at how much better your life has become.

A big expansion of the Ox career looks likely. A business Ox could be taking on more staff, quite a lot more staff. Employed Oxen, not currently managers, are likely to enjoy sudden promotion to management, which then involves recruiting more staff. Either way, you'll be surrounded by a growing band of new people. The Horse loves a herd.

What's more, flesh and blood Oxen often work in pairs, so it's quite likely you'll also team up with a like-minded colleague to work in close partnership. No need to frown. The two of you, pulling together, will be unbeatable. Before you know it, you'll have an empire, Ox.

If this sounds exhausting, don't worry, you can cope. Last year (though pleasing in so many ways) probably proved oddly tiring, though you couldn't quite work out why. This is because the dominant element of 2025 was Wood, and the Ox belongs to the Water tribe. Water feeds Wood, so it's no wonder Wood loves Water. But Wood's constant demands can drain Water's energy, and you end up feeling worn out and fatigued. You may even have been plagued by a succession of minor ailments – unusual for someone with a constitution as strong as yours.

Well, the good news, Ox, is that Wood's now leaving you in peace, and the fire element is sending your energy blazing back. New vitality will help you seize the goodies coming your way and put them to the best possible use.

Fire and water are not the easiest combination, of course, so you could encounter a lot of awkward situations and high-volume discussions. Most of these might appear dramatic at first, but will quickly fizzle out in a cloud of steam after a lot of hissing and stamping.

One area of discord could concern someone in your circle who's pressing for a major change in the Ox homestead. They may advocate a move to a distant area or even a different country. Naturally, you're not in favour, Ox. Yet the idea could grow on you. While you may not explore the suggestion this year, many an Ox could put it on the back burner and revisit it in 2027.

Another area of discord could be finance. You're the sensible type where cash is concerned, Ox. You don't spend unnecessarily, and money will be flowing in steadily this year. Yet someone in your orbit – either at home or at work – is burning through the budget like a crazed pyromaniac. You'll have to put a stop to it fast, Ox, or there'll be trouble. Yet once you've got your funds back under control, they'll grow pleasingly.

Finally, the Horse will ensure you do more travelling. You've got far too much work to have time for extended trips, many Ox will protest. Yet they manage to drag you away anyway. And you know what, Ox, you'll have a ball!

The Wonder of Being an Ox

Anyone who thinks being a zodiac Ox sounds a bit boring needs to think again.

Number two in the celestial River race – and only beaten to first place at the very last minute by the crafty rat – the essential, all-important Ox is highly regarded by the Chinese.

Never dismiss the Ox as simply a big cow with extravagant horns. In years gone by, the Ox was revered. It was thought so precious that it was viewed as a gift from the Gods. Rural life depended on the strength and endurance of the family Ox or Oxen if they were fortunate enough to have two. The beasts made a miraculous difference to farmwork and heavy jobs around the village. The community couldn't manage without them.

People born in the year of the Ox are renowned for similar qualities. In fact, it's believed in some quarters, that every workplace should have at least one Ox on board to ensure success. If you're typical of your sign, Ox, you're not all outward show and silly chatter. You embody serious, invaluable, genuine quality. You don't need to big up your worth or employ PR experts to polish your image. Your actions speak for themselves.

Oxen have a wonderful knack for planning a sensible, logical course to wherever they want to go and then following it, relentlessly, step by step, until they get there, no matter what obstacles they encounter enroute. Oxen find it rather puzzling that other people can't seem to adopt the same, simple approach. They don't understand why some signs give up before reaching their goal. Why do they waste their time chopping and changing and getting nowhere, wonders the Ox.

The stamina and endurance of the typical Ox is almost magical. People born under this sign can, if essential, work all through the night, pause for a quick shower and snack, and then go right back to the task. They'll do the same thing again the next night if the job demands it. And the next. Where other signs would crumble and break down, the Ox just plods on, impervious.

These people are the marathon runners of the universe. They are not built for speed, but then they don't need to be. They leave all that frenetic activity to the Monkey and the Rat. Sometimes, it's only patience and tenacity that will get a job done – and that's when only an Ox will do.

Okay, so you're not quite perfect, Ox. Who is? You're not known for your rapier wit or hilarious sense of humour. Though you enjoy a laugh as much as anyone, you're not permanently preparing the next joke or searching for the ironies of life. Survival is a serious business as far as you're concerned, and you intend to survive.

Then, you must admit, Ox, you can be stubborn. Call it tenacious if you like, and – of course – tenacity is a virtue, but it has to be said that when you make up your mind and dig your heels in, it would take dynamite to get you to budge.

Yet the Ox is genuinely honest, kind, and sincere, and not at all materialistic. In fact, the typical Ox is a born craftsman. People born under this sign will labour for hours for little financial gain, simply for the satisfaction of a job well done.

Finally, it takes a lot to seriously annoy the Ox, but when Ox gets mad, people tend to run. The Ox in a temper is a genuinely fearsome sight. Take cover. Better still, just don't go there.

The Ox Home

You have to know the Ox pretty well before being invited to the Ox home. The typical Ox is intensely private and wouldn't dream of inviting just anyone to their sanctuary. Get inside, though, and you will find a comfortable yet practical space filled with natural materials such as leather, wood, and stone. Bare of fripperies such as china ornaments, scented candles, and ruffled curtains, the Ox home may nevertheless be enlivened by some of Ox's own craftwork. Who knew Ox was so artistic? Carved driftwood, intricate collages, chunky jewellery, fused glass coasters – the Ox has mastered them all. Ox boasts green fingers, too, so sunny windowsills will be a tapestry of leaves and twigs as the latest Ox plant cuttings get underway. Just make sure you take a warm sweater when you visit. The temperature at the Ox home is kept notoriously low. Ox just doesn't feel the cold.

Being Friends with the Ox

It can take months, or even years, to be admitted to the Ox circle of trusted friends – which is usually tiny. This is because the typical Ox is a private, highly self-sufficient type. Ox has no need for dozens of different personalities jostling around. While the Ox is affectionate and enjoys company, this sign doesn't require constant companionship. Quiet 'me time' to recharge the Ox batteries is essential, plus the Ox is quite happy to be alone for extended periods. Yet, once admitted to the Ox group of special mates, you'll enjoy a loyal, caring friend who is keen to interest you in their latest artistic hobby or treat you to a mammoth picnic, ideally near water. On rare days off, the Ox loves to laze under the willows on a riverbank or make camp in the sand dunes of some wild beach. Just don't be offended if Ox is working too hard to socialise often, and be prepared for some surprisingly blunt comments. Ox doesn't understand sugar-coating reality and is notoriously plain-spoken. Yet adjust to the eye-wateringly frank Ox-speak, and you'll have a friend for life.

Ox Superpowers

Vast strength – both physical and mental

Stamina

Patience

Best Jobs for Ox 2026

Market Gardener

Accountant

Vet

Farm Manager

Chef

Perfect Partners

Cupid's arrow can strike anywhere at any time, of course, but once the novelty of new romance wears off, some relationships are easier to maintain than others. Here's a guide to the Ox's compatibility with other signs.

Ox with Ox

These two could be very happy together, as long as one of them plucks up the courage to admit they're interested. Sloppy, sentimental romance is not their style, and they both share this view so there'll be no misunderstandings around Valentine's Day. They know that still waters run deep, and they can enjoy great contentment without showy declarations of love.

Ox with Tiger

Not an easy match. Ox and Tiger could be on different planets. Fiery Tiger doesn't frighten Ox, and Tiger may admire Ox's strong, good looks and sincere nature, but they both need different things from life. Tiger wants to dash about changing the world for the better, while Ox reckons you get more done by buckling down where you happen to be and attending to the details. Clashes could abound.

Ox with Rabbit

Ox finds Rabbit rather cute and appealing. Whether male or female, there's something about Rabbit's inner fluffiness that brings out Ox's highly developed protective instincts. Rabbit meanwhile loves the Ox's reassuring presence and the sense of security Ox provides. These two could get on very well together as long as refined Rabbit can overlook Ox's occasional down-to-earth – Rabbit might say 'coarse' - observations.

Ox with Dragon

Chalk and cheese, though this pair may appear to be, there's a certain fascination between them. Ox may not approve of Dragon's showy manner but recognises Dragon's good intentions, while Dragon admires Ox's strength of character and gift for completing tasks. If each could find a way to tolerate the other's wildly different lifestyles, they might be good for each other, but in the long term, Dragon's hectic pace might wear even the Ox's legendary stamina.

Ox with Snake

Like Ox, the Snake is quietly ambitious and not given to racing around unless it's absolutely necessary. Ox, on the other hand, respects Snake's clever brain and understated elegance. These two could quickly discover how beneficial an alliance between them would be. They're both happy to give the other space when required but also step in with support when needed. This could be a very successful match.

Ox with Horse

Long ago, on many Western farms, Ox was replaced by the Horse, and it may be that Ox has never forgotten and never forgiven. At any rate, these two, despite both being big, strong animals, are not usually friends. Horse is too flighty and frivolous to interest Ox for long, while Ox's methodical, careful ways will irritate the Horse. Best not to go there.

Ox with Goat

Though these two share artistic natures (even if, in the case of the Ox, they're well hidden), deep down, they don't 'get' one another. Ox may be beguiled at first by Goat's friendly, easy-going manner but then disappointed to discover Goat seems to find everyone equally delightful, even those who are plainly unworthy. Goat, on the other hand, can't understand why Ox won't lighten up more. This relationship would require a lot of effort and compromise.

Ox with Monkey

The naughty Monkey scandalises Ox, but in such an amusing way that Ox can't help laughing. Monkey, on the other hand, is equally amused to find an audience that is so easy to shock. This unlikely pair enjoy each other's company and get on surprisingly well. Yet, right from the start, it's probably obvious to both that a long term relationship couldn't last. A fun flirtation, though, could be a terrific tonic for them both.

Ox with Rooster

For all its bravado and showing off, the Rooster is a down-to-earth type, drawn to security and accumulating the good things in life – requirements that Ox understands very well and can supply effortlessly. What's more, Ox can't help but admire Rooster's fine feathers and skill at communicating in a crowd – attributes Ox doesn't have and is unlikely to acquire. These two could enjoy a very good partnership.

Ox with Dog

These two ought to get along well as they're both sensible, down to earth, loyal and hardworking and in tune with each other's basic beliefs. And yet, somehow, they don't. Dog has a playful streak and finds this lacking in Ox, while Ox may be baffled by what seems like pointless silliness in Dog. If they can agree to differ, they could make a relationship work.

Ox with Pig

Delightful Pig will catch Ox's eye, and since Pig isn't a constant thrill-seeker, the two of them could enjoy many peaceful evenings together, perhaps over a tasty meal. Yet Pig's spendthrift ways – at least in Ox's eyes, could soon prove very annoying as well as illogical to the Ox, while Pig could find Ox's attitude judgemental and upsetting. Not ideal for the long term.

Ox with Rat

Oddly enough, this combination can be surprisingly successful. Frenetic Rat and calm Ox may seem to be opposites, but – in fact – Rat can find Ox's laid-back approach strangely soothing. Ox is not interested in competing with Rat and will patiently put up with Rat's scurrying after new schemes. As long as Rat doesn't get bored and generates enough excitement in other areas of life, this relationship could be very contented.

Ox Love 2026 Style

Ox would have you believe they've got no interest in faffing around with their hair or squeezing into some revealing outfit or prancing about in ridiculous shoes. How such nonsense could be fun is a mystery to Ox. And yet, when the typical Ox passes a mirror, they have been known to glance in. And be quietly pleased with what they see.

Yes, admit it, Ox. You're highly attractive when you make even the most minimal effort. You've got glorious hair, sparkling eyes, and a supple, athletic poise. Your healthy, wholesome, good looks would stop the traffic if you flaunted them a little more. Typical Ox dismisses such ideas as frivolous, of course.

Yet beneath that down-to-earth, plain-spoken exterior, the Ox hides a sensitive heart. Ox pretends not to care, but secretly, the typical bovine is a hopeless romantic. Single Ox is not inclined to play the field. Meaningless relationships seem, well, meaningless. So, what's the point? But that's because you're holding out for true love, aren't you, Ox? And the good news is, this year you could actually find it.

There's an intriguing, smouldering quality about you in 2026. Other signs sense passion lurking just beneath that calm, unruffled surface. They're desperate to draw closer to explore. So, this is not the time to get all defensive, Ox. Relax, bring out that charming smile, and give them a chance. You could be looking at your future soulmate.

Attached Ox could find life with their beloved a little unsettling. Things could be going very smoothly one minute then – without warning – your beloved throws a curve ball. Many Ox partners are feeling inexplicably restless this year and keen to make sweeping changes. Anything from painting the bedroom deep purple to six months trekking in Nepal is suddenly essential to their wellbeing. No point in asking why, Ox. Negotiate a compromise.

Secrets of Success in 2026

Uh oh. There's a bit of a Dragon feel to the Ox workplace right now. Just when you'd got your files sorted, the bills organised, your schedules properly worked out, and your diary straight, here comes the Horse to kick it all into disarray again.

This is the kind of thing that happened in 2024 when the boisterous Dragon was in charge and, if anything, the Horse is even worse.

You might as well just accept, Ox, that all your plans are going to change, then change again, and probably get altered or abandoned once more, right at the last minute. This is exactly the kind of thing that drives you crazy. It takes a lot to make you lose your temper, Ox, but this year the red mist could descend if you let it.

The Horse isn't intending to make you mad though. If you could step back, take a few deep breaths, and calm down, you might see that allowing more spontaneity into your life, and adopting a flexible approach, could magic ordinary, run-of-the-mill results into something special.

Comforting, practical routines can end up turning into chains that weigh you down, Ox. Get in touch with your inner wild Horse, break free this year, and watch your success rocket to a new level.

The Ox Year at a Glance

January – There's something about January that's so peaceful and full of promise. Get out your new calendar, assemble the holiday brochures, and make some to-do lists. Organisation is the key.

February – An annoying neighbour or new face in the workplace wants to rearrange things. Be polite, Ox.

March – A young person in your orbit has made a mistake, and now you have to rearrange a meeting. Don't explode, Ox. Make allowances. They're inexperienced.

April – The boss is piling on extra work all around. It's no problem for you. You might have to cover for the others, though.

May – You're being persuaded to try a blind date. Not your scene, Ox, but you could give it a try. What could possibly go wrong?

June – Someone close is feeling adventurous, and they want your support. Think it over.

July – Invitation after invitation arrives this month. What's going on? Who cares! Don't knock it, Ox. Say yes.

August – The Great Outdoors is calling. Make getting out in nature a priority.

September – Two tempting suggestions are put to you. Could be work related, could be romance. This is no time to play hard to get. Check them out.

October – Is it too late for an autumn break? Of course not. And why stick to one?

November – Someone in your circle is spending your hard-earned like it grows on trees. Time to read the riot act.

December – No point in pretending to be Scrooge. You know – deep down – that you love the festivities. Relax and put on that Santa outfit.

Lucky colours for 2026: Green, Red, Purple

Lucky numbers for 2026: 2, 7

Three Takeaways

Don't fuss
Seize the day
Think Fun

CHAPTER 10: THE TIGER

Tiger Years
13 February 1926 – 1 February 1927
31 January 1938 – 18 February 1939
17 February 1950 – 5 February 1951
5 February 1962 – 24 January 1963
23 January 1974 – 10 February 1975
9 February 1986 – 28 January 1987
28 January 1998 – 5 February 1999
14 February 2010 – 2 February 2011
1 February 2022 – 21 January 2023
19 February 2034 – 7 February 2035
6 February 2046 – 25 January 2047
24 January 2058 – 11 February 2059
Natural Element: Wood

Will 2026 be a Glorious Year for the Tiger?

Congratulations Tiger. You're one of the lucky winners of the *most fortunate sign of 2026 competition*. A very small, select band, as it happens. What do you mean you didn't enter any competition? You don't believe in competitions. You make your own luck, thanks. Well, like it or not, Tiger, you've been picked as one of the Crimson Horse's special favourites this year, so you might as well be grateful. You're the envy of the zodiac.

If you're typical of your sign, 2025 was probably not the easiest of years, Tiger. Such is your intelligence and drive, you've probably done well, despite provocations, but there have been a stream of annoyances that proved stressful along the way.

The trouble was all down to the fact that you and the Snake ruler of the year just don't gel. You're both smart and effective players, no doubt about it, but you operate in completely different ways. Where the Snake prefers to work quietly and unobtrusively from the shadows, you like to be out there in the full glare of day, fighting your battles openly and decisively. Yes, of course, you can stalk unseen for a while if absolutely necessary – you're a Tiger after all –but when it comes to the crunch, you leap out, identity crystal clear. You're brave and courageous. Skulking is not your style.

So, there were probably misunderstandings and differences of opinion aplenty in 2025. Yet you struggled on through and probably conquered them all.

Now, the good news for you in 2026 is that the Horse is completely different. Horse finds you interesting and exciting. Horse shares your 'can do' attitude and huge reserves of energy. What's more, the Horse loathes skulking in the background as much as you do. So, Horse energy can really help you go places this year, Tiger.

Right now, you can pick your favourite project, or three, and get them started. Yes, all of them. You have the ability to keep several balls in the air at once, and equine energy will hone you into a master juggler this year.

New businesses and new ideas crop up out of nowhere, and your magic touch conjures them into success in record time. Unfinished ventures from last year mature nicely and complete without further complications.

Employed Tigers are likely to encounter slightly more challenges. Ever the individual, it's difficult for the typical Tiger to follow another sign's lead. What's more, you don't suffer fools, do you Tiger, and there are plenty of fools crossing your path in 2026. So, a few explosive rows may enliven the big cat workplace. Yet when the blaze subsides and the smoke clears, you'll find you're the winner, and praise and rewards will swiftly follow, Tiger.

Oddly enough, when things are going well, typical Tiger gets restless. You're a rebel at heart, Tiger, and you need something to rebel against, or a cause to champion, to feel fulfilled. If these fail to materialise, you're quite likely to pick a fight with a supporter and sabotage your own interests, just to shake things up and give you something to protest about.

This instinct could be particularly strong in 2026 because the Horse shares a similar wild streak. Add to the mix the fact that it's a fire year, and you could be in danger of burning down the very thing you spent ages building up. Keep cool, Tiger; *bite your tongue and don't rise to any bait.*

Many Tigers will find a way to channel this energy into positive action to stop it from turning destructive. Under-rated charities, worthy causes, or local pressure groups may all catch the Tiger eye this year and benefit immensely from some big cat expertise. In fact, you could get so enthused that you end up turning a philanthropic side hustle into a full-time career.

Then there's the Tiger home. The typical Tiger doesn't much mind where they're based, as long as it's affordable and convenient for friends, family, and interests. So, this year, many a Tiger will find they've outgrown the old homestead and need to transfer their stuff elsewhere. It's unlikely to be a wrench moving on, though the typical Tiger loathes packing and sorting. But, by this time next year, many Tigers will have a new address. All good, Tiger. Discovering a new area and choosing fresh haunts will stimulate that lively mind.

As usual, money will come and go. Many Tigers could make quite a pile this year as more than one project looks likely to strike gold. Yet, somehow, the fiery energy surging around could burn a substantial hole in your stash. Unexpected expenses, essential equipment to buy, and – of course – new items for your new place… there's no avoiding the spending.

But will it get you down, Tiger? Not at all. You're having a blast.

The Wonder of Being a Tiger

How could it not be wonderful to be a Tiger? Big, bold, and beautiful, with a strong, athletic body, proud swagger and uncompromisingly individual style that manages to be magnificent yet strangely wild. People notice you, Tiger, and their jaws tend to drop. There is an awe-inspiring quality about you that they can't quite explain.

In China, the sign of the Tiger is regarded as fortunate and noble. The Tiger can't help but be a symbol of good fortune, of course, since in any jungle battle, the big cat is bound to come out on top. But the Chinese also emphasise a nobility about this sign.

Zodiac Tigers are fearless. They will fight with enormous courage, but their clashes are seldom for personal gain. Typical Tiger is prepared to battle to the death for a just cause, an abused underdog, or to defeat a tyrannical authority. The Tiger is a born revolutionary.

People born under this sign have been known to lose every penny they possess in the resulting struggle, but they don't really care. They're not materialistic. Money in the bank or frivolous knick-knacks mean little to them. If they have to sacrifice such trivialities for a good cause, it's worth it.

Yet the Chinese also believe the Tiger's stupendous, two-tone coat – the flaming orange, slashed with vivid stripes of darkest black – indicates a nature that has two sides.

Zodiac Tigers, while quite prepared to risk everything to aid a stranger in need, can turn surprisingly unsympathetic to close friends or relatives who've behaved foolishly.

What's more, the Tiger has an unpredictable temper and can change from purring pussy cat to snarling carnivore in an instant. Other signs tend to recognise this instinctively, and few will risk upsetting the big cat on purpose. Only the boldest Dragon or strongest Ox will dare tweak the Tiger's tail now and then.

Despite this, most Tigers are popular and charming. Their glamour and strength draws admirers to them, and – when things are going well – their inner kitten delights all companions. They know they can be a tad scary, so they keep their claws sheathed the majority of the time and collect a wide circle of loyal followers as a result.

Yet, somehow, and at some level, the Tiger always walks alone. Just as the Tiger doesn't really mind whether they have material goods or not, the big cat is also not fussed about having a companion along.

Tigers are great travellers; they're restless souls who hate to be in the same place for too long. So, the typical Tiger is always finding an excuse for another trip. Home or abroad, the Tiger doesn't mind just as long as they're on the move, although far-flung places do hold a special appeal to the big cat's imagination. And if a mate fancies joining Tiger on the Tiger's travels, that's fine; if not, the Tiger is just as happy to go alone.

This is a sign that scoffs at caution. Tigers take risks... every day. And the annoying thing, as far as their more wary zodiac cousins are concerned, is that the Tiger invariably escapes unscathed from situations where other signs would come severely unstuck. There's no doubt you're a lucky sign, Tiger, just don't forget cats only have nine lives.

The Tiger Home

Probably the most important item in the Tiger home is the Tiger passport. Followed by the Tiger suitcase, rucksack, and overnight bag.

The other thing about the Tiger abode, which visitors probably wouldn't notice at first, is that there's a handy escape route nearby. Easy access to a car, bus stop, or train station, plus an unobstructed front door, is essential. People born under this sign have to feel free.

Beyond that, the Tiger home is likely to be airy and furnished with clean lines and pale colours. Large windows and (where possible) bifold doors admit maximum light, and paintings and posters of greenery and outdoor scenes brighten the walls. The typical Tiger likes growing things but doesn't bother with houseplants unless there's someone to water them while Tiger's away. The same goes for pets.

The typical Tiger isn't much interested in housework or cooking either, so the kitchen is little used and the fridge is bare, but there's a dishwasher if possible. Tiger does invite the occasional guest now and then and entertains them with takeaway meals and generous glasses of the latest exotic brew brought back from Tiger's travels. Somehow, it all hangs together, and visitors are happy to return.

Being Friends with the Tiger

It's not always easy being friends with the Tiger. Magnetic and original, the Tiger attracts admirers, and people feel rather privileged to be admitted to the big cat's inner circle. What's more, as a Tiger friend, you'll never be bored; lively Tiger has an endless stream of entertaining tales and extraordinary info picked up on their trips. Plus, the Tiger has always got a project or an exciting new place to explore lined up, and friends are welcome to get involved. The Tiger's not at all clingy and expects little from you in return.

Yet, the Tiger can be moody. One day, they're the sunniest of souls; the next, grouchy and uncommunicative. They always seem to be falling out with someone, too, for reasons that are unclear. And then, just as you're beginning to get to know them better, they're going away again and they're not sure when they'll be back.

So, it's great to be friends with a Tiger as long as you don't need a shoulder to lean on or a regular companion for your own interests.

Tiger Superpowers

Stunning presence

Fearless

Devotion to justice

Best Jobs for Tiger 2026

Military

Actor

Safari Park Guide

Food Bank Manager

Aid Worker

Explorer

Perfect Partners

Cupid's arrow can strike anywhere at any time, of course, but once the novelty of new romance wears off, some relationships are easier to maintain than others. Here's a guide to the Tiger's compatibility with other signs.

Tiger with Tiger

The attraction between these two beautiful people is powerful. They understand each other so well; it's almost like looking in a mirror. They both like to walk on the wild side and will enjoy some exciting adventures together, but their moody interludes could lead to fierce quarrels. This match could be compulsive but stormy.

Tiger with Rabbit

Surprisingly, the Rabbit is not intimidated by Tiger's dangerous aura, and this attitude immediately appeals to Tiger, who enjoys a challenge. Rabbit's calm presence and clever way with words keeps Tiger interested, while Rabbit finds Tiger's adventurous tales entertaining. With care, these two could get on well together for years.

Tiger with Dragon

The two biggest personalities in the zodiac would seem bound to clash. After all, these larger-than-life characters share so many similarities there's a danger they'd compete. Yet a relationship between the Tiger and Dragon often works very well. They understand each other's impulsive natures, but they're also different enough to supply the support the other needs. They'd make a formidable power couple.

Tiger with Snake

Not the best of romances. These two are so fundamentally different that any initial attraction is unlikely to last. Snake likes to bask and conserve energy, while Tiger wants to leap right in and race about. Tiger takes in the big picture in a glance and is off to the next challenge, while Snake likes to pause, delve beneath the surface, and consider. It wouldn't take long before these two annoy each other.

Tiger with Horse

This athletic pair get on pretty well. They both like physical pursuits, testing their strength out of doors or just enjoying the feel of the wind in their hair and the ground under their feet. True, Horse may not quite understand Tiger's plans for world domination, but it doesn't really matter. Horse is happy to be loyal to such a charismatic partner. As they're both moody, there could be rows, but making up is exciting.

Tiger with Goat

Tiger and Goat don't have a lot in common. While their aims and temperaments are quite different, they are both sociable creatures, and Goat wouldn't mind Tiger attracting all the attention when they're out together. Tiger, in return, would appreciate Goat's lack of jealousy and generosity of spirit. Yet, in the long term, they're likely to drift apart as they follow their different interests.

Tiger with Monkey

Tiger can't help being intrigued by sparkling Monkey, and Monkey is flattered by such interest. Who wouldn't enjoy being admired by such a fabulous creature? But irrepressible Monkey just can't help teasing, and being teased is not a sensation Tiger is familiar with nor appreciates. Unless the attraction is very strong, these two will wind each other up until they can bear it no longer and part.

Tiger with Rooster

The only feathered creature in the zodiac, the opulence and novelty of Rooster's appearance will draw Tiger like a magnet. What's more, deep down, they are both quite serious-minded types, so – on one level – they'll have much to share. Yet, despite this, they're not really on the same wavelength, and misunderstandings will keep recurring. Could be hard work.

Tiger with Dog

While not exactly opposites, these two are different enough to intrigue each other yet similar enough in basic outlook to get on well. Both Tiger and Dog are idealistic and uninterested in material gain, yet where Dog can be nervous, Tiger is bold; and where Tiger attracts controversy, Dog will be loyal. This partnership could be lasting and valuable.

Tiger with Pig

Carefree Pig will love to bask in Tiger's impressive aura, while Tiger will feel good about protecting this charming but unworldly creature. They enjoy each other's company and Tiger, so focused on lofty matters, will find Pig's compulsive shopping too trivial to worry about.

This couple could do well together as long as Pig's fondness for cosy nights in doesn't make Tiger feel trapped.

Tiger with Rat

Sleek and clever Rat can easily attract Tiger's attention because the intelligent Tiger loves witty conversation. Yet, these two are not natural partners. Tiger's not interested in Rat's latest bargain and has no wish to talk about it while Rat doesn't share Tiger's passion for changing the world. Still, if they can agree to step back and not get in each other's way, they could reach a good understanding.

Tiger with Ox

Not an easy match. Ox and Tiger could be on different planets. Fiery Tiger doesn't frighten Ox, and Tiger may admire Ox's strong, good looks and sincere nature, but they both need different things from life. Tiger wants to dash about creating big changes, while Ox reckons you get more done by buckling down where you happen to be and attending to the details. Clashes could abound.

Tiger Love 2026 Style

It's really not fair, Tiger. You're drop-dead gorgeous with a devastating yet faintly dangerous edge to your charm. As well as your dramatic good looks, there's that slow, sensual way of strolling around you have when you're relaxed that just hypnotises other signs. They reckon you're glamour in motion – and they're not wrong. They can't take their eyes off you.

Basically, you never have to try, Tiger. You only have to raise an approving eyebrow, or lift a beautifully manicured finger, and the partner of your choice comes running. It's no different this year, Tiger. If anything, you've got even more admirers drooling over you, bathed as you are in the radiance of Horse's specially favoured sign.

Chances are, you don't even realise how fortunate you are, or that other signs don't possess your appeal.

On the other hand, one of the great things about the single Tiger is they're broad-minded. They don't insist on a particular type – they're prepared to give any suitably enthusiastic admirer a chance. Unfortunately for the admirer, though, very few can live up to Tiger's exacting standards. Single Tiger never intends to be a heart-breaker, but somehow can't seem to stay with the same date for long.

So, will you settle down this year, Tiger? Probably unlikely. But you'll be in your element auditioning the candidates.

Attached Tigers probably don't realise how rare they are. It's not easy to pin a Tiger down for long. Your beloved is obviously a clever operator who knows just how to keep you challenged and prevent you from becoming bored. Go along with whatever they suggest this year, Tiger. Passions are high. You won't regret it.

Secrets of Success in 2026

Success is actually seeking you out this year, Tiger. The restless energy of the Horse is just waiting to seize your projects and accelerate them away towards the stratosphere. Everything you set in motion should grow and grow fast in 2026. But energetic as you are, it might be difficult even for you, Tiger, to keep up with it all.

What's more, this is a Fire year, and you are a Wood creature. Fire loves Wood and seeks you out for obvious reasons. Everything you do right now will attract attention, that's for sure. Yet too much Fire can exhaust Wood's reserves. You could literally burn out if you're not careful.

You've got such a strong constitution you're not used to needing to pace yourself, Tiger, but this year – even though there are so many exciting opportunities coming your way – you need to slow down. Take frequent breaks, spend time in nature, and be picky over where you devote your time. Just remember, you can do a lot, but *you can't do everything*. Activate that discriminating eye, select your projects with care, and you can't lose.

The Tiger Year at a Glance

January – Still on your travels or about to leave? Either way, you discover something interesting.

February – An appealing new face seems keen on romance. No harm in getting to know them better.

March – Typical Tiger hates house hunting, but sometimes there's no choice. Don't accept the first thing that comes along. Check out the competition.

April – A former boss has reappeared in a new role. Will it affect you? Only in a good way.

May – Stubborn types are twitching your tail. You could eat them all for breakfast, but resist retaliation, Tiger. Think patience and restraint.

June – This is more like it. A noble cause is brought to your attention. Can you help? No question.

July – Charity begins at home. Just as you're about to launch into something new, assistance is required in the family circle. Good thing you can multitask.

August – Some of your ventures are really taking off. You're onto something big. Pace yourself, Tiger.

September – A career project whisks you across water. Good news. You love to travel.

October – An old flame gets in touch. You'd almost forgotten them, but they haven't forgotten you. Time for a revisit?

November – A colleague fancies mixing business with pleasure. Not normally your thing, but on the other hand, what's the harm?

December – Is it possible to do Christmas Eve in one place, the big day in another, followed by Boxing Day miles from either? Of course it is, Tiger. Check for transport complications, though.

Lucky colours for 2026: Blue, Grey, White

Lucky numbers for 2026: 4, 1, 5

Three Takeaways

Pace yourself
Get picky with projects
Don't be sarcastic to the boss

CHAPTER 11: THE RABBIT

Rabbit Years
2 February 1927 – 22 January 1928
19 February 1939 – 7 February 1940
6 February 1951 – 26 January 1952
25 January 1963 – 12 February 1964
11 February 1975 – 30 January 1976
29 January 1987 – 16 February 1988
6 February 1999 – 4 February 2000
3 February 2011 – 22 January 2012
22 January 2023 – 9 February 2024
8 February 2035 – 27 January 2036
26 January 2047 – 13 February 2048
11 January 2059 – 1 February 2060
Natural Element: Wood

Will 2026 be a Glorious Year for the Rabbit?

Okay Rabbit, time to polish up that charming smile, sort out your most flattering threads, and clear your diary as much as possible. You're about to become extremely popular. People are going to notice you this year, Rabbit, and it's no good trying to slide out of the spotlight… attention will find you wherever you hide.

Some signs, of course, would be thrilled at a prospect like this. Basking in the limelight would be a dream come true. But if you're typical of your sign, Rabbit, you're a sensitive, modest type, and being thrust centre stage is more like a nightmare than a wish come true. When it comes to public scrutiny, less is more as far as you're concerned.

So, chances are, you're going to view 2026 with mixed feelings.

Last year, under the benign eye of the Snake, most Rabbits enjoyed an agreeable time. Yes, there were probably a few unexpected curve-balls – the Snake just can't help itself – but generally you and the Snake get on well. The Snake approves of your understated competence and refusal to show off. While you find the quieter atmosphere produced by the serpent to be soothing and encouraging. Rabbit ventures tend to flourish when life is calm.

But now it's all change again, and if you just *know* 2026 is set to be different, you're right. What we're looking at here, Rabbit, is a double whammy, as far as peaceful bobtail is concerned, of a spirited Horse ruler combined with a Fire year.

Why should this combination be daunting? For a start, the Horse and the bobtail are not the greatest of friends. Horse doesn't dislike you Rabbit, it is just that Horse's broad-brush approach fails to mesh well with your devotion to finesse and detail.

So, right away, Horse energy is trying to rush you into completing tasks long before you consider them finished or make decisions while you are still collating the necessary facts. This irritates you, Rabbit.

Then, more importantly, last year was a Wood year and you're a Wood creature, so you were instinctively in sympathy with the prevailing mood, without even trying. This year, however, is completely different. 2026 is a Fire year, hosting fire in its strongest form. On top of that, the Horse belongs to the Fire tribe. So, this year, you have double Fire to contend with, Rabbit. That fiery element will be racing through 2026 like a runaway train.

Not only is Fire all about speed, action, and change – three things that make the typical Rabbit shudder – it also loves Wood. Fire is literally hungry for you, Rabbit. It seeks you out. You can't hide away. It finds you wherever you go and wants you to stay and play. You're more inclined to do the opposite, but Fire needs Wood to keep on burning, and it won't let go.

This magnetic attraction could play out in day-to-day life as an endless stream of opportunities showering every corner of the bobtail life. A deluge of customers for the business Rabbit, piles of work, and extra responsibility for the employed Rabbit. New offers, head-hunters messaging you, previous contacts getting back in touch… in fact, important decisions to be made everywhere you turn, and they all want more, more, more.

One or two of these things could be viewed as wonderful, Rabbit, but when there are too many it's just overwhelming. Yet there's a danger, if you try to ignore the onslaught or delay your response, that situations could blow out of control and turn destructive.

It's similar at home. Somehow, everyone in the Rabbit clan is clamouring for attention. If you're typical of your sign, Rabbit, you may be called upon to settle bobtail disputes, assist in bobtail finances, oversee domestic improvements, and organise bobtail transport. Oh, and don't forget that holiday they're all looking forward to.

No, there's absolutely no chance of hibernating for 12 months, Rabbit, so don't even go there. The point is, if you manage to ride these boisterous waves, if you keep your head and refuse to panic, 2026 could turn out to be the most splendid time for Rabbit's future prospects in decades.

And maybe because you're so indispensable to Fire, many a Rabbit will be thrown a lifeline this year to help them cope.

At home, family members and old friends will come forward offering help. At work, you'll get the chance to delegate. This is not the time to come over all proud and independent, Rabbit, and refuse. Accept all the aid you can get your hands on. Resist the urge to criticise if they fail to meet your exacting standards. The job may not get done as well as you would have done it, Rabbit, but at least it will get done. And this year, that's what's going to count.

Yes, things could get stressful. Yes, there will be times when you feel like walking away from it all. Yet by the time the new year comes around again, you'll realise you've had a fantastic time.

The Wonder of Being a Rabbit

Star of many an Easter card and welcome emblem of Spring, the gentle Rabbit offends no one – unless you happen to be a market gardener, of course.

Basically, everyone loves the cuddly bunny; so harmless a creature it's regarded as the perfect toy for the tiniest baby. The Chinese associate the zodiac Rabbit with good luck as well as peace and harmony. The most admirable of qualities.

Yet don't be fooled by that softest of soft fur and the cute little powder puff bobtail. The Rabbit may come over as timid and vulnerable, but in fact it's a great survivor. Wherever Rabbits thrive, there are tireless predators, yet the defenceless Rabbit mostly evades them all and manages to hop on, multiplying regardless. Along with the Rat, the Rabbit is an incredibly successful species.

People often underestimate you, Rabbit, with your soft voice, quiet appearance, and perfect manners – yet you are much tougher than you look. And, of course, if you're typical of your sign, Rabbit, you usually find this quite useful. Rivals tend to let their guard down around the unthreatening Rabbit – a mistake from which clever Rabbit unobtrusively benefits.

Vulgarity is almost physically painful to the true bobtail. Rabbits are instinctively classy with cultured tastes. They love art, restraint in all things, and order. Messy surroundings, eye-searingly clashing colours, loud noises, and pungent smells make them feel ill. Raised voices and torrid quarrels, meanwhile, can bring on a migraine.

No wonder the sensitive Rabbit strives for harmony above all else. People born under this sign are the peacemakers of the universe. They have a knack for persuading the most bitter of enemies to agree to compromise. They refuse to take sides, see everyone's point of view, quell discord, and somehow wind up friends with all parties.

Rabbits are such born diplomats they really should consider applying to the government for a professional role. No one has to teach Rabbit to be tactful or discreet. These qualities are written through the bobtails, like the letters through a stick of rock.

What's more, the typical Rabbit always finds the perfect words for every occasion. They're never pushy but they know just what to say to nudge situations the way they want them to go. They are such brilliant strategists – possibly because the bunny, having no physical means to defend itself, is forced to get by on wits alone. For this reason, people born under this sign usually rise to the top of whatever profession they happen to have chosen, leaving their colleagues scratching their heads as to how they achieved it.

Yet, as satisfying as career success may be, the true Rabbit's real passion is family. Family comes first as far as Rabbit is concerned, and if all is well with the loved ones, Rabbit is content.

The Rabbit Home

You're in for a treat if you get invited to the Rabbit home. Only the most favoured guests are wafted across the Rabbit threshold because the bobtail warren is a precious sanctuary. But should you be trusted enough to get inside, you'll find a beautifully decorated, softly lit space with a wonderfully soothing atmosphere. Harmonious colours (naturally) blend perfectly into each other, the walls resemble an art gallery, and tasteful objects are displayed in just the right places to catch the eye but not jar. There are often quite a few children in residence, yet somehow the place remains miraculously tidy. The

Rabbit is a wonderful host and guests are spoiled with dainty nibbles and the finest beverages, while the bobtail children tumble about delighting everyone with their innocent charm. You can't wait to go back.

Being Friends with the Rabbit

Since the Rabbit gets on with everyone, it's more difficult not to be friends with the Rabbit. Yet there are friends, and then there are *real* friends. Rabbit probably doesn't realise it, but most of the Rabbit friends could more properly be classed as friendly acquaintances. Rabbit has dozens of these: workmates, business associates, neighbours, and people Rabbit met on the school run. Yet the *real* friends tend to be small in number and have known Rabbit for years. These are the people Rabbit feels completely at ease with and is happy to see at any time. They probably met at school or university and have shared all life's ups and downs ever since. But whichever category you fall into, the point is that Rabbit will never annoy you and should you annoy the Rabbit, you'll likely never find out. Reduce the chances of this, if possible, by removing your shoes on entering the Rabbit abode, refraining from all criticism, never speaking in harsh tones and – above all – avoiding arguments with any of Rabbit's guests. Keep to these rules, and you'll never be crossed off Rabbit's Christmas card list.

Rabbit Superpowers

Supreme tact

Discretion

Perfect taste

Best Jobs for Rabbit 2026

Antiques Restorer

Interior Designer

Fashion Model

Artist

Diplomat

HR Consultant

Family Support Worker

Perfect Partners

Cupid's arrow can strike anywhere at any time, of course, but once the novelty of new romance wears off, some relationships are easier to maintain than others. Here's a guide to the Rabbit's compatibility with other signs.

Rabbit with Rabbit

These two gorgeous creatures look like they're made for each other. Their relationship will always be calm, peaceful, and unruffled, and it goes without saying that their home could grace a glossy magazine. Yet, though they never argue, the willingness of both partners to compromise could end up with neither ever quite doing what they want. Ultimately, they may find the spark goes out.

Rabbit with Dragon

Dragon is such a larger-than-life character, Rabbit could feel overwhelmed at times. Also, the Dragon can be rather noisy and overdramatic, which would get on Rabbit's nerves. Yet they each admire the other's good points. If they could live next door to each other instead of under the same roof, a long-term relationship might work.

Rabbit with Snake

This subtle pair could make a good combination. They both understand the value of working behind the scenes, and neither has any desire to wear themselves out on endless adventures. They share a love of art, fine things, and quiet pleasures, and they both enjoy an orderly home. These two could settle down very happily together.

Rabbit with Horse

This could be tricky. It's fairly unlikely that Horse and Rabbit would ever end up on a date, but if they did, and there was a strong attraction, it could lead to a love/hate relationship. Rabbit's neat and tidy ways would enrage Horse, and Horse's unpredictable moods and over-the-top reactions would annoy Rabbit. Soon, Horse is likely to bolt for the hills or Rabbit retreat to its burrow.

Rabbit with Goat

Happy-go-lucky Goat is very appealing to Rabbit, particularly as deep-down Rabbit is a bit of a worrier. They're both sociable without needing to be the centre of attention and would be happy to people-watch for hours and then cheerfully compare notes afterwards. Goat is tolerant of Rabbit's need for some regular alone time to recharge, too, so this couple could be a successful match.

Rabbit with Monkey

Mercurial Monkey doesn't really 'get' Rabbit. The Monkey can appreciate how well Rabbit operates and sees this approach gets good results, but it's all too picky and slow for Monkey. Rabbit, on the other hand, is amused by Monkey's quick wit and clever ways but deplores Monkey's slapdash, sometimes devious tactics. Very unlikely to work out.

Rabbit with Rooster

Another difficult match. However unfair it seems, Rooster comes over as loud, boastful, and uncouth to Rabbit, while Rabbit appears dull, staid, and insufficiently admiring of Rooster's fine feathers to appeal to Rooster. These two just can't see below the surface of the other, and it would be surprising if they ended up together. Only to be considered by the very determined.

Rabbit with Dog

Despite the fact that in the outside world, Rabbit could easily end up as Dog's dinner, the astrological pair get on surprisingly well. Dog appreciates Rabbit's careful, efficient ways and soft voice, while Rabbit admires Dog's energy and good intentions. Dog's lack of interest in the finer points of interior design might try Rabbit's patience, but with a little work, these two could reach an understanding.

Rabbit with Pig

Pig is not quite as interested in fine dining as Rabbit, being as happy to scoff a burger as a Cordon Bleu creation, but their shared love of the good things in life makes these two happy companions. Once again, Pig's spending habits might irritate Rabbit, but not too much, as Rabbit is quite willing to splurge on lovely things for the home. A relationship would work well.

Rabbit with Rat

Rat finds Rabbit intriguing. Here is an attractive, stylish creature that doesn't feel the need to be pushy or take centre stage, yet somehow manages to be at the heart of things, while Rabbit is flattered and entertained by witty Rat's attention. These two respect each other but, in the long term, Rat could be too overpowering unless they both agree to give each other space.

Rabbit with Ox

Ox finds Rabbit rather cute and appealing. Whether male or female, there's something about Rabbit's inner fluffiness that brings out Ox's highly developed protective instincts. Rabbit, meanwhile, loves the Ox's reassuring presence and the sense of security Ox provides. These two could get on very well together as long as refined Rabbit can overlook Ox's occasional down-to-earth – Rabbit might say 'coarse' – observations.

Rabbit with Tiger

Surprisingly, the Rabbit is not intimidated by Tiger's dangerous aura, and this attitude immediately appeals to Tiger, who enjoys a challenge. Rabbit's calm presence and clever way with words keeps Tiger interested, while Rabbit finds Tiger's adventurous tales entertaining. With care, these two could get on well together for years.

Rabbit Love 2026 Style

Whoever said 'If you've got it, flaunt it' was most definitely not a Rabbit. And they weren't talking about a Rabbit, either. The vulgarity of such a sentiment is enough to make the typical Rabbit pale in horror.

True Rabbits never willingly draw attention to themselves, yet there's something about their elegant good looks, exquisite clothes, and quiet dignity that turns every head in every room they enter. Rabbit exudes class, effortlessly. Quality is written through them like the letters through a stick of rock. They're never pushy or demanding, seldom raise their voices, and are usually to be found at any gathering, hovering serenely in a discreet corner.

Yet even in a mundane year, despite your natural modesty, Rabbit, you nevertheless exert a mysterious magnetic appeal. Somehow, other signs are drawn helplessly to your side and once there, are very reluctant to move.

But this year, with the full radiance of the firelight dancing around you, lighting you up like a West End stage, you just can't fail. Your aura glows so bright that admirers are completely dazzled. If you're not careful, they'll fall at your feet and then – kind Rabbit that you are – you'll feel obliged to pick them up and look after them. Romance is certainly not going to be a problem for the single Rabbit. Just make sure you don't stay too long in a relationship that's going nowhere.

Attached Rabbits can look forward to a year of passion! Your partner's all fired up and can't wait to entice you into the burrow. No point in fighting it, Rabbit. Enjoy…

Secrets of Success in 2026

You might well be thinking, Rabbit, that just to get to the end of this year in one piece will count as success. Well, stop being so pessimistic. Actually, your prospects have seldom been brighter. You'll encounter a deluge of mouth-watering opportunities courtesy of the Horse – all you've got to do is figure out how to take advantage of them.

This will involve applying that clever bobtail brain to the challenges that arise and refusing to give in to your famous tendency to 'freeze in the headlights' when the going gets stressful. Emotion is not your friend right now. You need to be cool and dispassionate and weigh up each contingency, logically.

Quite early on, it should become clear you can't do everything yourself. There's either too much work, or you don't have the necessary expertise, or the deadline's way too short, or you don't have the funds. It might be all four. Yet the only way to stop the Horse galloping off, taking your good fortune with it, is to bring in outside assistance.

Don't be stubborn about admitting you need help. Just take the time as soon as possible to assemble Team Rabbit. Pick trusted faces with the expertise you lack, plus others who are happy and skilled enough to share your workload. It's probably wise at the moment to avoid untried new people and opt for colleagues and acquaintances you already know, who've proved reliable in the past.

Once Team Rabbit steams into action, you'll be amazed at the success pouring your way. This little band is so effective that chances are you'll stay together for decades. By the end of 2026, many a Rabbit will be wondering why they didn't do this years ago.

The Rabbit Year at a Glance

January – Decorations are coming down in the Rabbit home, and it's looking bare. Time to go shopping.

February – There's a sudden upturn at work, but you have to act fast. Can you meet the new deadlines? Keep calm.

March – Minor ailments in the Rabbit orbit. Have you got time to run around playing nurse? No option but to multitask.

April – Someone stamping around and making a fuss – at home or at work. Maybe both! Don't stand for any nonsense, Rabbit. Stick to your rules.

May – You've caught someone's eye, and they're interested in you. We're not talking business here. Is romance out of the question?

June – An old friend is making plans to leave for distant shores. You fear they're making a mistake. Should you assist or persuade them to stay?

July – A partner reckons it's time for a break. You can't wait, but you're so busy. Can you get ready in time?

August – The colony is gathering. You try to get together every year if possible. Complicated diary rearranging required.

September – Someone in the workplace is trying to muscle in on your plans. Put your foot down, Rabbit.

October – Bill, bills, bills, but then a breakthrough. A big win or an unexpected payment is coming your way.

November – Yay! That extra cash means you can start your shopping early. Go for it, Rabbit.

December – Romantic Christmas plans get steamy. A festive season to remember.

Lucky colours for 2026: Pink, Jade, Indigo

Lucky numbers for 2026: 3, 6, 8

Three Takeaways

Get help
Don't be stubborn
Flexibility is key

CHAPTER 12: THE DRAGON

Dragon Years

23 January 1928 – 9 February 1929
8 February 1940 – 26 January 1941
27 January 1952 – 13 February 1953
13 February 1964 – 1 February 1965
31 January 1976 – 17 February 1977
17 February 1988 – 5 February 1989
5 February 2000 – 23 January 2001
23 January 2012 – 9 February 2013
10 February 2024 – 28 January 2025
28 January 2036 – 14 February 2037
14 February 2048 – 1 February 2049

Natural Element: Wood

Will 2026 be a Glorious Year for the Dragon?

Yay! Good news, Dragon. Looks like you're on a roll. 2026 is set to be another of those years where your natural brilliance gets the chance to shine and dazzle all bystanders – just the way it should.

If you're honest, Dragon, you've probably missed the limelight that illuminated you so spectacularly back in 2024. Back then, you were ruler of the year, everyone had to do things your way, and admiring eyes clocked your every move. Fortunately, you've never been the shy type, so you adored the attention.

It must have come as a bit of an anti-climax then, when your mate – the Snake – took over last year and you were forced to hand in your crown. To be honest, many Dragons were relieved at first. There was so much excitement and drama in 2024 that it drained the resources of even the strongest of fire-breathers. So, if you're typical of your sign, Dragon, in 2025 you were probably glad of the chance to rest on your laurels, polish up your well-earned hoard, and quietly build on your past achievements. The friendly Snake was delighted to help you consolidate your enviable position.

Yet even before the Snake slithered off, chances are you were getting restless, Dragon. There's only so much downtime a Dragon can tolerate before they start feeling bored, and you probably hit that dull spot long before the serpent disappeared.

Well, you can crack open the champagne now, Dragon, because that's all about to change. Here comes the Horse to fire things into action again. While you and the Horse are not total besties, you share the same dynamic approach and love of the spotlight. You both like to be out in front, going places, making things happen. And in 2026, the Horse is going to help you get back in the race, and then some.

That's not to say it'll be easy, Dragon. The Horse will put many hurdles in your path for the sheer fun of seeing you leap them. But Horse forgets Dragons have wings. You'll soar swiftly over every obstacle, Dragon, and rise to even greater success. It's an absolutely thrilling challenge as far as the Dragon's concerned.

This year, many Dragons will start a new business or special project. Possibly something that's been on the fire-breather's mind for some time. Other Dragons may resurrect a cherished venture from the past that's been simmering on the back burner for too long. The Horse will help speed all such bold moves to the finish line.

Employed Dragons could find further recognition at work and be given new areas to conquer. Your leadership skills have never been in doubt, Dragon, and they'll be called upon now.

As a result of all this growth, cash will be flowing in at great speed. Chances are, it won't hang around long in the Dragon coffers, though. Many Dragons will be more interested in investing their stash than saving in a conventional style. Property of some kind could come Dragon's way in 2026, a new home, a caravan by the sea, or even a fancy tent will suddenly become overwhelmingly tempting.

Intriguingly, it looks as if many Dragons will catch the eye of some mentor or benefactor in 2026. This mystery person expects great things of you, Dragon. You have their total confidence, and their influence is likely to help you for years to come. Try not to upset them!

Overall, the main challenges likely to be encountered by the typical Dragon this year are down to the combination of 2026 being a Fire year and the Horse ruler being a Fire creature. Double Fire causes events to race along so fast you can hardly catch your breath.

If anyone can keep up, you can, Dragon, but you can't afford to lose concentration for a second or events could spiral out of control. What's more, the fiery energy restores your confidence so well that your self-belief could go over the top, and you end up making poor decisions because you're certain you're never wrong.

The other thing to bear in mind is you're a Wood creature, Dragon, which is why Fire loves you so much. You are the perfect fuel. Fire can't wait to be around Wood creatures like you for obvious reasons. While you're happy to provide what Fire needs for a while, eventually, the constant demands get too draining. To avoid exhaustion, you must set firm boundaries this year, Dragon.

In day-to-day life, you may have to turn down a few enticing offers and tell the family or that expanding social circle you can't attend every gathering or finance every unexpected bill. You're the generous type, Dragon, but even you have to put limits on your time and your money.

All in all, Dragon, 2026 will be an exhilarating year for you. Wins galore will thrill your competitive nature, wealth will pour in, and there'll be enough challenges to keep you interested. What Dragon could wish for more?

The Wonder of Being a Dragon

You really are quite annoying, Dragon. No wonder the other signs are secretly envious of you. You might think that being the only mythical creature in the zodiac was a disadvantage, but no, you've got it all.

Good looks, charm, strength, talent, energy. Plus, of course, the Chinese regard you as the luckiest sign of the lot, not only enjoying a fortunate life yourself but also bringing good luck to the family in which you were born.

No wonder the birth rate in Chinese communities rises noticeably in a Dragon year. Everyone wants a Dragon baby if it's physically possible.

The typical Dragon is enthusiastic, extroverted, totally honest, and incredibly energetic. In fact, you're a bit overpowering for some of the more low-key signs, Dragon. In true Dragon style, though, you probably don't even notice.

Dragons mean well. They have so many gifts they take their good fortune for granted. Full of optimism and creativity and buzzing with ideas, they dash about enlisting support for their latest project – and getting it – without even realising they've not finished the last.

Point this out, and Dragon's likely to shrug good-naturedly and assure everyone that everything's in hand.

These people think BIG and have a gift for inspiring others, but they get bored easily and quickly move on to the next adventure when the previous one gets tedious.

The typical Dragon is a bit of a star and usually rises to the top of whatever workplace they find themselves in. They make excellent leaders, but only if they have a good number two at their side. A Snake, for instance. This is because while the Dragon excels at the big picture, the all-important picky details tend to make their eyes glaze over. They really can't be bothered, and this trait often gets them into trouble.

Yet the Dragon is seldom without cash for long – despite the risks they can't help taking. Their obvious gifts attract money and they frequently end up wealthy. Bafflingly to other signs, though, the typical Dragon is not particularly interested in an overflowing bank account and is not motivated by money – though they will accept any contributions offered.

No, what gets the Dragon up in the morning is a new goal, a tempting adventure, or just being in on the action. A Dragon without a cause, a plan, or an idea to explore is a very depressed Dragon indeed.

Dragons are friendly and kind-hearted and can be suckers for a hard luck story. They'll give generously to someone in need and can be relied on to do the right thing, even if it's against their own interests. Yet they get so carried away with their own enthralling plans they can be surprisingly insensitive to the people around them.

But what other signs don't realise is that for all its confidence, the Dragon is easily hurt. Reject the Dragon, and Dragon will withdraw for days, deeply wounded, although too proud to admit it. What a complicated sign you are, Dragon.

The Dragon Home

The public rooms in the Dragon home are likely to be light, airy, and feature very large windows. Dragons like to be able to see as much sky as possible. Should the property also overlook water, Dragon is unlikely ever to move. Yet few visitors get to admire the Dragon abode since most Dragons are far too busy for mundane tasks such as housework. They tend to acquire so much 'stuff' in connection with their latest project that the majority of surfaces are covered with brochures, papers, and sundry pieces of equipment. There isn't really room for guests. Dragon would much rather meet friends and relatives in the nearest pub or coffee shop. The few guests that get past the door will receive a warm welcome, however, as long as they don't mind clearing a space for themselves on the nearest sofa and making their own cup of coffee in the kitchen. Probably making one for Dragon while they're at it, too. What no one will see (except the closest of relatives) is the dim little room hidden away at the back: the Dragon lair. Stuffed with soft cushions, places to sprawl, and thick curtains, this is where Dragon retreats when things get too much even for the mighty Dragon.

Being Friends with the Dragon

The Dragon loves friends and tends to collect quite a few, so it's easy to strike up a friendship with people from this sign. The trouble is they're so busy and have such an extensive network, they're likely to forget about you. They're such fun to be with and such stimulating company, however, you probably won't mind, but you'll have to be prepared to do all the running and make the effort to stay in touch. What's more, in any circle, the Dragon can't help ending up being the centre of attention. They don't intend to dominate, but somehow, they just do. This is fine for most signs content to bask in Dragon's entertaining glow. Yet others find this behaviour insufferable. Should you be a zodiac Tiger or Dog, you may find extrovert Dragon too much to take. And then there's the way the cheerful Dragon can suddenly turn morose and disappear alone for extended periods for no apparent reason. They'll never talk about it, but some slight or other thing has hurt their feelings. Leave them be, though, and after a while they'll bounce back as if nothing's happened.

Dragon Superpowers

Confidence

Enthusiasm

Creativity

Best Jobs for Dragon 2026

President

Actor

General

Barrister

Screenwriter

Sales Executive

Creative Director

Politician

Perfect Partners

Cupid's arrow can strike anywhere at any time, of course, but once the novelty of new romance wears off, some relationships are easier to maintain than others. Here's a guide to the Dragon's compatibility with other signs.

Dragon with Dragon

When Dragon meets Dragon, onlookers tend to take a step back and hold their breath. These two are a combustible mix – they either love each other or loathe each other. They are so alike, it could go either way. Both dazzling in their own orbits, they can't fail to notice the other's charms, but since they both need to be centre stage, things could get competitive. With give and take and understanding, this match could work well, but it won't be easy.

Dragon with Snake

Surprisingly, this couple gets along beautifully. Snake's elegant appearance and quick but subtle mind intrigues Dragon, while Snake admires Dragon's success and endless energy. Snake has no need to battle for the limelight and is quite happy to sit back and support Dragon's schemes from the comfort of a stylish sofa. Which is all the encouragement Dragon needs.

Dragon with Horse

The athletic Horse is pretty good at keeping up with dashing Dragon. And Dragon appreciates a partner who enjoys getting out and about as much as Dragon does. Yet Horse might grow weary of Dragon's constant new projects and resent having to be involved. Horse likes to go off and do Horsey things at frequent intervals, which Dragon tends to view as disloyal. This relationship could get fiery.

Dragon with Goat

Goat tends to baffle the busy Dragon. Dragon can see Goat is the creative type but can't understand why Goat doesn't appear to be working very hard when so much could be achieved. In fact, if they stayed together long enough, Dragon could help Goat make the most of many talents, but it's unlikely either of them can sustain enough interest for this to happen.

Dragon with Monkey

These two are likely to hit it off immediately. Each is attracted to the other's intelligence and lively presence, and Dragon's exuberance doesn't overwhelm hyperactive Monkey. What's more, though they both enjoy being surrounded by a crowd, Monkey only wants to make people laugh, while Dragon hopes to inspire them to a cause. There is no conflict, so this couple can help each other to go far.

Dragon with Rooster

A Dragon and Rooster pairing will always attract attention. These two are both gorgeous beings and love to be surrounded by admirers. They will probably enjoy going out together and being seen as a couple, but in the long term, they may not be able to provide the kind of support each secretly needs.

Entertaining for a while, but probably not a lasting relationship.

Dragon with Dog

Not the easiest of combinations. Down-to-earth Dog can't see what all the fuss is about when it comes to Dragons. Unimpressed by glamour and irritated by what seems to Dog the gullibility of Dragon admirers, Dog can't be bothered to find out more. Dragon, meanwhile, is hurt by Dog's lack of interest. Great determination would be needed to make this work.

Dragon with Pig

While Dragon and Pig might seem to be opposites, the two of them can create a surprisingly contented relationship. Pig is quite happy for Dragon to fly around doing exciting things as long as Pig is not expected to do much more than admire profusely. Dragon appreciates Pig's uncritical support and makes allowances for Pig's lack of stamina. This couple could live in harmony.

Dragon with Rat

This couple is usually regarded as a very good match. They have much in common, being action-loving, excitement-seeking personalities who hate to be bored. It takes a lot to dazzle Rat, but the Dragon's glamorous aura proves irresistible, while Dragon loves to be admired, so each enjoys being with the other. There could be the odd power struggle as these two are both strong characters, but the magnetism is so intense they usually kiss and make up.

Dragon with Ox

Chalk and cheese, though this pair may appear to be, there's a certain fascination between them. Ox may not approve of Dragon's showy manner but recognises Dragon's good intentions, while Dragon admires Ox's strength of character and gift for completing tasks. If each could find a way to tolerate the other's wildly different lifestyles, they might be good for each other but, in the long term, Dragon's hectic pace might wear down even the Ox's legendary stamina.

Dragon with Tiger

The two biggest personalities in the zodiac would seem bound to clash. After all, these larger-than-life characters share so many similarities there's a danger they'd compete. Yet a relationship between the Tiger and Dragon often works well. They understand each other's impulsive natures, but they're also different enough to supply the support the other needs. They'd make a formidable power couple.

Dragon with Rabbit

Dragon is such a larger-than-life character, Rabbit could feel overwhelmed at times. Also, the Dragon can be rather noisy and overdramatic, which would get on Rabbit's nerves. Yet they each admire the other's good points. If they could live next door to each other instead of under the same roof, a long-term relationship might work.

Dragon Love 2026 Style

You're so hot this year, there are practically flames coming off you, Dragon. Always the star of any production, you're so accustomed to admirers trailing in your wake that you hardly notice them. You just assume they were heading in the same direction as you.

For this reason, you're not the type to agonise too much over your appearance either. In fact, you barely notice those few imperfections. They make no difference to your appeal, so why fuss? But when a frivolous mood strikes and you dress up for the sheer fun of it, you're probably amazed and a little puzzled to find other signs practically queuing for your autograph.

So, this year, Dragon, you can expect to be a show-stopper. Walk into any room and you'll be surrounded by eager fans in seconds. Your glamour is legendary, but in 2026, it hits a new, high-octane level.

Single Dragons will be forced to turn away a series of disappointed admirers, but it's a bit like Whack-a-Mole. The more you reject, the more will bob up in their place. Yet despite basking happily in all the attention, you'll only have eyes for one special person. Give them all the time they want, Dragon. You won't be sorry.

Attached Dragons could find their beloved extra demanding, in a good way. They want more of your attention, Dragon; they'd like you to spoil them a little. Put your phone away, turn off the TV, and think 'couple time'.

Secrets of Success in 2026

Sounds easy, doesn't it, Dragon? Leap aboard the galloping Horse, hang on tight, and let it dash you across the finishing line to glittering success and wild acclaim. That's in your dreams, of course.

In reality, as you well know, there's a lot more to it than that. Even with the Horse ready and willing to assist, you've got to put in the sustained effort over quite a long period in order to reap any rewards.

The key word here is 'sustained', Dragon. Effort is no problem for you. You're positively eager to begin a project and throw your considerable energies at it for hours on end. But you must admit, Dragon, that you can be impatient. You also have a tendency to get bored easily. If the results take too long to show themselves, it isn't long before a new venture catches your eye and you're tempted to transfer your efforts in a different direction.

This has been the downfall of many a promising Dragon project in the past, but it's a particular danger in 2026. The Horse is as impatient as you are, and will encourage you to zoom off to pastures new the second any venture seems to drag. Ignore such appealing impulses and get in touch with your inner Ox, Dragon. You've got the stamina in there for the long haul if you put your mind to it, and you'll be amazed at the success your projects will generate if you complete them properly.

Finally, keep an eye out for that unexpected benefactor. They may be someone you already know, or they could be a new face, but whoever they are, they're going to give your future prospects a wonderful boost.

The Dragon Year at a Glance

January – You're still in the mood for dancing, Dragon. Is it too late to sign up for a class?

February – A mystery card arrives on February 14. Who can it be from? Fun finding out.

March – Trainees in the workplace are put in your care. As if you haven't got enough to do. Flattering though, Dragon.

April – An exciting offer comes your way. Can you manage this? Have faith, Dragon.

May – Unexpected cash has your name on it. Did you win the lottery? You didn't buy a ticket? It might be the time to start.

June – A project that was taking too long suddenly streaks ahead. This is more like it, Dragon. Don't lose concentration.

July – You're off shopping for a big purchase. Don't be too rash. Think this over carefully.

August – A crazy friend is holding a surprise party. You're sworn to secrecy. Keep your mouth shut, Dragon.

September – Countryside or by the ocean – it looks like you'll be tempted away. The fresh air will do you good.

October – A relative has got into difficulties. Their finances are a disaster. Unless you're an accountant, Dragon, keep out of it.

November – the Dragon stash is growing beautifully, but you can think of so many ways to spend it. Save some for a rainy day.

December – A lively Christmas somewhere new, Dragon. Don't overdo the mince pies.

Lucky colours for 2026: Navy, Silver, Emerald Green

Lucky numbers for 2026: 7, 8

Three Takeaways

Stay focussed

Network

Make time for fun

CHAPTER 13: THE SNAKE

Snake Years
10 February 1929 – 29 January 1930
27 January 1941 – 14 February 1942
14 February 1953 – 2 February 1954
2 February 1965 – 20 January 1966
18 February 1977 – 6 February 1978
6 February 1989 – 26 January 1990
24 January 2001 – 11 February 2002
10 February 2013 – 30 January 2014
29 January 2025 – 16 February 2026
15 February 2037 – 3 February 2038
2 February 2049 – 22 January 2050

Natural Element: Fire

Will 2026 be a Glorious Year for the Snake?

Phew Snake. What a year! You must be exhausted. This might be a good time to have a lie down, pour yourself a calming beverage, and lock the door on any well-meaning friends or family who fancy a chat.

You were in charge in 2025, and if you're typical of your sign, Snake, you couldn't be more pleased to pass on the crown. It's all very well being the boss, but after a while, all that planning and organising wears you out. You're probably very happy your zodiac cousin – the Horse – has taken over. Horse is welcome, as far as you're concerned.

Despite the fact that you and Horse are not particularly fond of each other, the prospect of a Horse year doesn't faze you, Snake. While the Horse might be slightly nervous of you, you're pretty relaxed around the Horse. This probably stems from some ancient memory of the way your celestial namesake sneaked across the river, wound round Horse's leg, and beat Horse to the shore. You know that – should the need arise – you can handle the Horse. There's nothing to fear from the big equine.

Last year, there's no doubt you achieved a lot. The celestial Snake uncovered no end of scandals, conspiracies, and general skullduggery. Events unfolded in extraordinary and unexpected ways. People put it down to coincidence but you knew better!

On a personal level, if you're typical of your sign, you've overseen a great many improvements in the Snake orbit. Quite a few serpents are now basking in new premises and contemplating interesting career choices.

2026 is going to help you consolidate all these gains and maybe grow some more. When you're ruler of the year, you often manage to lay down interesting foundations but end up too busy to have much time to build on them.

Now, with the invigorating energy of the Horse powering you on, Snake, you can put that right. In 2026, you can start building those beginnings into mighty prospects.

Business Snakes will find orders and offers expanding in a very pleasing way. Employed Snakes discover that their uncanny efficiency last year has impressed people in high places. Promotion, new roles, and added responsibility are likely to be showered on you, Snake. Plus, the opportunity to diversify into an area you'd never considered before.

You can expect extra funds to swell the Snake coffers too – not just through increased earnings but possibly through a win or a gift from a generous partner.

The great thing about this year is that it's a Fire year, and you belong to the Fire clan. You instinctively understand the prevailing atmosphere and can ride its peaks and troughs with ease. The Horse may be too hasty and over-emotional for your refined tastes, Snake, but you have a knack for extracting the equine's useful characteristics, discarding the rest, and going quietly on your way without the Horse even noticing what you've borrowed.

The only problem – as far as the typical Snake is concerned – is that the restless speed of the Horse doesn't suit your constitution. Snake energy tends to come in short, intense bursts followed by rest, while the Horse gallops on tirelessly for hours. In the coming year, offers, situations, and events are likely to unfold at a pace that's unsettling for serpents. What's more, many Snakes are still fatigued after the efforts of 2025.

You're likely to feel an overwhelming need to rest and relax in 2026, Snake. Consequently, many Snakes will be enjoying a series of wonderful holidays. Hot and sunny, luxurious and indulged, or maybe just lounging in a leafy garden, you can look forward to them all. Don't let other signs criticise you for extravagance or suggest you're being lazy. You need to recharge and should grab every opportunity.

There's also the chance many a Snake will take up a new hobby that could develop into a lifestyle change. From yoga to Japanese cooking, from jewellery-making to jiu-jitsu, an intriguing new pastime could turn into a passion. Soon, you could be making alterations to your décor or social life to accommodate the latest obsession. Home gym? New kitchen? Outside workshop? It's all possible, Snake.

Snakes that were too busy to make the move or home improvements they wanted last year are likely to get a second chance in 2026. The pressure's off and you've now got some space to browse, check out what's on offer, and make up your mind. Horse energy will try to rush things, of course, but sensible Snake will refuse to be coerced. Insist on taking your time, and you'll come up with a gem.

If you're typical of your sign, Snake, you're pretty self-contained, but this year friends, relatives, and colleagues could impinge on your tranquillity. And not in a good way. Many of them are all fired up in a negative fashion by the heated atmosphere. Rows and sudden flare-ups are likely to explode without warning, and they're inclined to take things out on you. Foolish of them, really, Snake. That cool serpent exterior conceals inner fire. You can give as good as you get, Snake… better in fact! You'll put them in their place in a trice. They won't pick on you again in a hurry!

All in all, you can look forward to 2026 with confidence. Just sit back and watch Snake's fortunes blossom.

The Wonder of Being a Snake

Come on, admit it. You always knew you were a bit special, didn't you, Snake? Perhaps at some point then, deep down, you were a little dismayed to find your sign was the Snake. How could this be, you might think, when you're such a delightful person? But you probably only feel that way because it's in the West that the Snake gets very bad press.

The very name can be an insult, and people tend to shudder and back away from the real-life creature.

Yet this attitude is to misunderstand the sheer brilliance of this extraordinary beast.

Imagine a creature that has no legs yet can shoot across the ground with lightning speed; a creature that, when peckish, can swallow an animal many times its own size in one gulp; a creature that, when annoyed, can spit venom across a forked tongue; a creature that, for an encore, can slip out of its entire skin to present a brand new, wrinkle-free body beneath.

It sounds so magical; it's difficult to believe such a creature really exists. Yet that's the miracle we call a Snake.

The Chinese have long recognised the exceptional gifts of the Snake, and for this reason, in the East, the sign of the Snake is highly respected.

It's associated with wisdom, intelligence, grace, and renewal. The Chinese also believe it's a sign of great beauty, and it's true that most people born under the sign of the Snake have a distinctive poise and attractiveness that draws people to them, even if they're not conventionally beautiful. They are also blessed with a natural grace of movement. They're born dancers with a great appreciation for music.

The Snake is highly intuitive, sometimes psychic too, and perhaps this – along with their mystical link to renewal and rebirth – is the reason for the Snake's long reputation for healing. They instinctively 'know' what ails a person and how to make them feel better, though chances are they couldn't tell you where this knowledge comes from.

Despite all these gifts, the typical Snake is a little reserved. Their restrained manner is often mistaken for shyness. Yet the Snake is not exactly shy, more intensely private. People born under this sign prefer to sit on the sidelines, quietly observing and giving nothing away until they startle everyone with their astute summing up of the situation. They are also excellent readers of character, and it's very unwise to lie to a Snake. That penetrating gaze will see straight through falsehoods, and should you lose the trust of a Snake, you're unlikely to get it back, ever.

Strangely enough, despite their modest behaviour, the Snake has a reputation for great ambition – due to the creature's determination to swallow prey larger than itself, usually successfully.

For this reason, Snakes have an amazing ability to rise to the top of any career ladder, without apparently making much effort. In fact, at work, some Snakes are even assumed to be chronically lazy because they appear to do as little as possible. What their colleagues fail to realise is that the Snake tires easily and needs to conserve energy as much as possible. While capable of great speed and stamina, the Snake only employs such effort when it's absolutely essential. The rest of the time, Snake works smart rather than hard – but because the Snake is smarter than most, this is usually more than adequate.

The other remarkable thing about people born under this sign is that they'll patiently put up with all manner of unpleasantness and unfavourable situations seemingly forever and then suddenly – snap. They walk away without warning or a backward glance, leaving onlookers stunned.

Only afterwards do people learn that the Snake has been inert and silently brooding for months. But it's no good imploring Snake to return. Snake's actions are swift and irrevocable.

The Snake Home

The Snake home is a special place. Most Snakes need a private sanctuary where they can relax completely and mull over the events of the day, the week, and probably the last ten years. Snakes are great 'mullers' – given to brooding if they don't get out enough.

They also need a tranquil space where they can plot their next move uninterrupted. They're great plotters and planners, too, and prefer to have events thought out in advance.

Those privileged to be invited to the Snake home will find a tasteful, beautifully arranged hideaway with an accent on comfort and clean lines. They may be surprised, too, to discover the quiet Snake is an unexpectedly excellent host. The finest food and drink will be pressed on guests, and visitors will be encouraged to entertain and gossip. Gossip is particularly enjoyed by the Snake. A fun evening is guaranteed – just don't expect to be invited back too often.

Being Friends with the Snake

The Snake makes a loyal and mostly undemanding friend, but they give their friendship sparingly. Intensely private people, it takes a while for them to admit new faces to their inner circle, and even when they do, it's unlikely they will confide all their secrets, ever. Nevertheless, they will support and aid their friends with genuine care. Don't take advantage, though. The Snake tends to see things in black and white. Annoy the Snake (surprisingly easy to do, though you might never know they were upset) or worse, lie to them, and they will cut you off instantly.

Snake Superpowers

Spooky intuition

Can persuade anyone to do anything

Razor-sharp insight

Best Jobs for Snake 2026

Designer

Gymnast

Editor

Historian

Florist

Counsellor

Reflexologist

Perfect Partners

Cupid's arrow can strike anywhere at any time, of course, but once the novelty of new romance wears off, some relationships are easier to maintain than others. Here's a guide to the Snake's compatibility with other signs.

Snake with Snake

This fine-looking couple turn heads wherever they go. Beautiful and perfectly dressed, these two look like the perfect match. They never stop talking and enjoy the same interests, so this could be a successful relationship. Long-term, however, there could be friction. They're both experts at getting what they want using the same sophisticated techniques, so they can see through each other.

Snake with Horse

At some level, perhaps, Horse remembers how Snake beat him in the calendar race, so despite an initial attraction, these two could be wary of each other. Snake is impressed by Horse's energy and athleticism, while Horse admires Snake's elegance and charm. Yet they don't really have much in common. Deep-thinking Snake could find Horse rather shallow, and Horse may see Snake as frustratingly enigmatic.

Snake with Goat

Snake and Goat could enjoy many happy hours touring art galleries and exhibitions together. Neither of them craves excitement and harsh, adrenaline-boosting activities, and both appreciate creative artistic personalities. There's no pressure to compete with each other, so these two would sail along quite contentedly. Not a passionate alliance, but they could be happy.

Snake with Monkey

These two clever creatures ought to admire each other if only for their fine minds and, at first, it's possible they might. But unless they're really determined to make it work, it won't be long before active

Monkey finds Snake's energy-saving ways irritating, while Snake loses patience with Monkey's endless jokes.

Snake with Rooster

Surprisingly, Snake and Rooster work well together. Both are gorgeous in different ways; they complement each other without competing. Snake's keen eyes can see beneath Rooster's proud facade to the sensitive, unsure person inside, while Rooster appreciates Snake's unobtrusive strength and wise words of encouragement at just the right moment. These two could be inseparable.

Snake with Dog

Some Snakes seem to have an almost hypnotic power and, for some reason, Dog is particularly susceptible to these skills. We've heard of snake charmers, but snakes can be dog charmers and, without even trying, Snakes can find themselves the recipients of Dog devotion. Since the Dog is strong, loyal, and can be fun, Snake is not averse to this but might, in the end, find it boring.

Snake with Pig

Pig and Snake don't have a lot to say to each other. Snake can't be bothered with Pig's endless shopping, and Pig is hurt by Snake's snobbish attitude. They both enjoy the good things in life, so a luxury fling could briefly be fun – a shared spa break might be a good idea – but in the long term, this relationship is probably not worth pursuing.

Snake with Rat

The Snake shares Rat's good taste, and being elegant, sophisticated, and smart will delight Rat at first sight. These two get on very well on an intellectual level, but perhaps are better as good friends rather than long-term partners. The Snake's love of basking in the sun for hours strikes Rat as lazy and dull, while Rat's need to rush around doing deals and meeting people seems pointless and wearying to Snake.

Snake with Ox

Like Ox, the Snake is quietly ambitious and not given to racing around unless it's absolutely necessary. Ox, on the other hand, respects Snake's clever brain and understated elegance. These two could quickly discover how beneficial an alliance between them would be. They're both happy to give the other space when required but also step in with support when needed. This could be a very successful match.

Snake with Tiger

Not the best of romances. These two are so fundamentally different that any initial attraction is unlikely to last. Snake likes to bask and soak up the sun, while Tiger wants to explore and discover. Tiger takes in the big picture at a glance and is off to the next challenge, while Snake likes to pause, delve beneath the surface, and consider matters. It wouldn't take long before these two annoy each other.

Snake with Rabbit

This subtle pair could make a good combination. They both understand the value of working behind the scenes, and neither has any desire to wear themselves out on endless adventures. They share a love of art, fine things, and quiet pleasures, and they both enjoy an orderly home. These two could settle down very happily together.

Snake with Dragon

Surprisingly, this couple gets along beautifully. Snake's elegant appearance and quick but subtle mind intrigues Dragon, while Snake admires Dragon's success and endless energy. Snake has no need to battle for the limelight and is quite happy to sit back and support Dragon's schemes from the comfort of a stylish sofa. Which is all the encouragement Dragon needs.

Snake Love 2026 Style

The question the other signs are dying to ask, Snake, is 'do you realise how sexy you are?'. You're so silent and enigmatic at times, while simultaneously displaying such a knowing glint in your eye, they can't make out whether you're deliberately beguiling or totally unaware of the effect you have.

Hmmm. Given the power of that inscrutable brain, Snake, it's probably fair to say you know exactly what you're doing. Even Snakes not blessed with conventional good looks exercise an almost hypnotic appeal. There's something about the graceful, unhurried way you move, your supple, yet elegant physique, and the way you don't just sit in a chair but uncoil, languorously and melt into the cushions, that drives other signs wild.

The other maddening thing about you, Snake, is you play so hard to get. Which only makes admirers want you more. Except, of course, the Snake is not playing. The typical Snake is well aware of serpent worth and doesn't bestow it lightly. The Snake partner has to be a worthy contender or Snake is not remotely interested. And single Snakes are quite content to make themselves comfortable and conserve their energy until Mr or Ms Right shows up.

So, this year, Snake, you're as sizzling as ever. Possibly more so in the reflected glory of the double fire year. You might just deign to entertain one or two hopeless cases simply because you're in a good mood but, of course, they don't stand a chance. Yet you never know…

an unexpected romance on one of those holidays this year could surprise you. You may just meet a worthy partner after all.

Attached Snakes in a relationship with another fiery sign could have a blistering year.

Secrets of Success in 2026

Prepare to go up in the world, Snake. Your astonishing feats last year have not gone unnoticed and the rewards are just beginning to filter through. Keep on doing what you're doing and success will find its way unerringly to you. You don't have to work too hard to be a star right now.

Crucial this year, though, is your need to rest and pace yourself. Many Snakes are unaware of quite how drained they've become from their efforts in 2025. Even if you don't feel too fatigued, it makes sense to relax in 2026 as much as possible. And Snakes that already notice a sensation of weariness should organise some R & R as a priority.

Fortunately, the fiery Horse is lending you extra oomph, so you'll bounce back more quickly than usual, but make sure you include plenty of downtime in your schedule all year.

The other way of preserving the serpent constitution is to shut out the energy vampires in your orbit. You don't have a lot of patience with time wasters in the normal run of things, Snake, but now you need to cut them out completely.

Acquaintances or colleagues who detain you on the phone, or by your desk with trivia, can be politely encouraged to go elsewhere. Friends or family members who confuse you with an Agony Aunt must be avoided at all costs, and instead of trying to decipher complicated rules, regulations, or operating instructions yourself, call in an expert. Save effort wherever you can, Snake, and you'll be amazed how good you feel.

You could even do a personal stress audit and make a list of all the places you can save hassle. Shopping – get it delivered. Housework – hire a cleaner. Drive to work – carshare. Exercise the dog – find a dog walker. Social media – turn off your phone. Okay, so investments may need to be made in some areas, but as the serpent wealth grows, you can afford it, Snake.

Put all this into operation, and you'll feel like a brand new Snake by the time the Horse gallops away.

The Snake Year at a Glance

January – You don't like the cold, Snake. Check out the sales and invest in some extra cosy alpine gear.

February – A fiery face is generating heat in the workplace. Doesn't bother you, Snake, but others are intimidated. No need for conflict. Lead by setting a cool example.

March – The Snake residence is looking a little tired. Time to study the paint charts.

April – A past love shows up and wants to rekindle your romance. You could be tempted, Snake. Think it over.

May – Renovations chez Snake are going well. You don't like to get your hands dirty, but if you want a job done…

June – Someone in the family circle is organising a trip. It sounds a little risky. No, you don't want to accompany them.

July – A pay rise could have your name on it. How soon will you get the cash? Don't spend it too soon, Snake.

August – Everyone's off on holiday and you're thinking of joining them. Think sunshine, Snake. The warmer the better.

September – Can you take on more responsibility, Snake? Someone in authority is counting on you. Could you? Should you?

October – A young relative needs your expertise, Snake. Very difficult to refuse.

November – Party time gets earlier and earlier in the Snake orbit. You're tempted, though. Time to buy something sparkly.

December – The family's aiming for your place, Snake. You pretend to sigh, but you love it really. Best Christmas tree in the street.

Lucky colours for 2026: Purple, Black, and Orange

Lucky numbers for 2026: 5, 8, 9

Three Takeaways

Chill
Switch off your phone
Refuse to argue

CHAPTER 14: BUT THEN THERE'S SO MUCH MORE TO YOU

So now you know your animal sign, but possibly you're thinking – okay, but how can everyone born in the same year as me have the same personality as me?

You've only got to think back to your class at school, full of children the same age as you, to know this can't be true. And you're absolutely right. What's more, Chinese astrologers agree with you. For this reason, in Chinese astrology, your birth year is only the beginning. The month you were born and the hour of your birth are also ruled by the twelve zodiac animals – and not necessarily the same animal that rules your birth year.

These other animals then go on to modify the qualities of your basic year personality. So, someone born in an extrovert Tiger year but at the time of day ruled by the quieter Ox, and in the month of the softly spoken Snake, for instance, would very likely find their risk-taking Tiger qualities much toned down and enhanced by a few other calmer, more subtle traits.

By combining these three important influences, you get a much more accurate and detailed picture of the complex and unique person you really are. These calculations lead to so many permutations it soon becomes clear how people born in the same year can share various similarities, yet still remain quite different from each other.

What's more, the other animals linked to your date of birth can also have a bearing on how successful you will be in any year and how well you get on with people from other signs. Traditionally, the Horse and the Rabbit are not best buddies, for instance, so you'd expect two people born in these years to be unlikely to end up good friends. Yet if both individuals had other compatible signs in their charts, they could find themselves surprisingly warming to each other.

This is how it works:

Your Outer Animal – (Birth Year | Creates Your First Impression)

You're probably completely unaware of it, but when people meet you for the first time, they will sense the qualities represented by the animal that ruled your birth year. Your Outer Animal and its personality influence the way you appear to the outside world. Your Outer animal is your public face. You may not feel the least bit like this creature deep down, and you may wonder why nobody seems to understand the real you. Why is it that people always seem to underestimate you, or perhaps overestimate you, you may ask yourself frequently. The reason is that you just can't help giving the impression of your birth-year animal and people will tend to see you and think of you in this way – especially if they themselves were born in other years.

Your Inner Animal – (Birth Month | The Private You)

Your Inner Animal is the animal that rules the month in which you were born. The personality of this creature tells you a lot about how you feel inside, what motivates you, and how you tend to live your life. When you're out in the world and want to present yourself in the best light, it's easy for you to project the finest talents of your birth-year animal. You've got them at your fingertips. But at home, with no one you need to impress, your Inner Animal comes to the fore. You can kick back and relax. You may find you have abilities and interests that no one at work would ever guess. Only your closest friends and loved ones are likely to get to know your Inner Animal.

By now you know your Outer Animal so you can move on to find your Inner Animal from the chart below:

Month of Birth - Your Inner Animal

January – the Ox

February – the Tiger

March – the Rabbit

April – the Dragon

May – the Snake

June – the Horse

July – the Goat

August – the Monkey

September – the Rooster

October – the Dog

November – the Pig

December – the Rat

Your Secret Animal – (Birth Hour | The Still, Small Voice Within)

Your secret animal rules the time you were born. Each 24-hour period is divided into 12, two-hour time-slots and each slot is believed to be ruled by a particular animal. This animal represents the deepest, most secret part of you. It's possibly the most intimate, individual part of you as it marks the moment you first entered the world and became 'you'. This animal is possibly your conscience and your inspiration. It might represent qualities you'd like to have or sometimes fail to live up to. Chances are, no one else will ever meet your Secret Animal.

For your Secret Animal check out the time of your birth:

Hours of Birth – Your Secret Animal

1 am – 3 am – the Ox

3 am – 5 am – the Tiger

5 am – 7 am – the Rabbit

7 am – 9 am – the Dragon

9 am – 11 am – the Snake

11 am – 1.00 pm – the Horse

1.00 pm – 3.00 pm – the Goat

3.00 pm – 5.00 pm – the Monkey

5.00 pm – 7.00 pm – the Rooster

7.00 pm – 9.00 pm – the Dog

9.00 pm – 11.00 pm – the Pig

11.00 pm – 1.00 am – the Rat

When you've found your other animals, go back to the previous chapters and read the sections on those particular signs. You may well discover talents and traits that you recognise immediately as belonging to you in addition to those mentioned in your birth year. It could also be that your Inner Animal or your Secret Animal is the same as your Year animal. A Dragon born at 8 am in the morning, for instance, will be a secret Dragon inside as well as outside, because the hours between 7 am and 9 am are ruled by the Dragon.

When this happens, it suggests that the positive and the less positive attributes of the Dragon will be held in harmony, so this particular Dragon ends up being very well balanced.

You might also like to look at your new animal's compatibility with other signs and see where you might be able to widen your circle of friends and improve your love life.

CHAPTER 15: IN YOUR ELEMENT

There's no doubt about it: Chinese astrology has many layers. But then we all recognise that we have many facets to our personalities, too. We are all more complicated than we might first appear. And more unique, as well.

It turns out that even people who share the same Chinese zodiac sign are not identical to people with the same sign but born in different years. A Horse born in 1966, for instance, will express their Horse personality in a slightly different way to a Horse born in 1978. This is not simply down to the influence of the other animals in their chart, it's because each year is also believed to be ruled by one of the five Chinese 'elements', as well as the year animal.

These elements are known as Water, Wood, Fire, Earth, and Metal.

Each element is thought to contain special qualities which are bestowed onto people born in the year it ruled, in addition to the qualities of their animal sign.

Since there are 12 signs endlessly rotating, and five elements, the same animal and element pairing only recurs once every 60 years. Which is why babies born in this 2026 Year of the Crimson Horse are unlikely to grow up remembering much about other Crimson Horses from the previous generation. Those senior Crimson Horses will already be 60 years old when the baby Crimson Horses are born.

In years gone by, when life expectancy was lower, chances are there would only ever be one generation of a particular combined sign and element alive in the world at a time.

Find Your Element from the Chart Below:

The 1920s

5 February 1924 – 24 January 1925 | RAT | WOOD

25 January 1925 – 12 February 1926 | OX | WOOD

13 February 1926 – 1 February 1927 | TIGER | FIRE

2 February 1927 – 22 January 1928 | RABBIT | FIRE

23 January 1928 – 9 February 1929 | DRAGON | EARTH

10 February 1929 – 29 January 1930 | SNAKE | EARTH

The 1930s

30 January 1930 – 16 February 1931 | HORSE | METAL

17 February 1931 – 5 February 1932 | GOAT | METAL

6 February 1932 – 25 January 1933 | MONKEY | WATER

26 January 1933 – 13 February 1934 | ROOSTER | WATER
14 February 1934 – 3 February 1935 | DOG | WOOD
4 February 1935 – 23 January 1936 | PIG | WOOD
24 January 1936 – 10 February 1937 | RAT | FIRE
11 February 1937 – 30 January 1938 | OX | FIRE
31 January 1938 – 18 February 1939 | TIGER | EARTH
19 February 1939 – 7 February 1940 | RABBIT | EARTH

The 1940s

8 February 1940 – 26 January 1941 | DRAGON | METAL
27 January 1941 – 14 February 1942 | SNAKE | METAL
15 February 1942 – 4 February 1943 | HORSE | WATER
5 February 1943 – 24 January 1944 | GOAT | WATER
25 January 1944 – 12 February 1945 | MONKEY | WOOD
13 February 1945 – 1 February 1946 | ROOSTER | WOOD
2 February 1946 – 21 January 1947 | DOG | FIRE
22 January 1947 – 9 February 1948 | PIG | FIRE
10 February 1948 – 28 January 1949 | RAT | EARTH
29 January 1949 – 16 February 1950 | OX | EARTH

The 1950s

17 February 1950 – 5 February 1951 | TIGER | METAL
6 February 1951 – 26 January 1952 | RABBIT | METAL
27 January 1952 – 13 February 1953 | DRAGON | WATER
14 February 1953 – 2 February 1954 | SNAKE | WATER
3 February 1954 – 23 January 1955 | HORSE | WOOD
24 January 1955 – 11 February 1956 | GOAT | WOOD
12 February 1956 – 30 January 1957 | MONKEY | FIRE
31 January 1957 – 17 February 1958 | ROOSTER | FIRE
18 February 1958 – 7 February 1959 | DOG | EARTH
8 February 1959 – 27 January 1960 | PIG | EARTH

The 1960s

28 January 1960 – 14 February 1961 | RAT | METAL
15 February 1961 – 4 February 1962 | OX | METAL
5 February 1962 – 24 January 1963 | TIGER | WATER

25 January 1963 – 12 February 1964 | RABBIT | WATER
13 February 1964 – 1 February 1965 | DRAGON | WOOD
2 February 1965 – 20 January 1966 | SNAKE | WOOD
21 January 1966 – 8 February 1967 | HORSE | FIRE
9 February 1967 – 29 January 1968 | GOAT | FIRE
30 January 1968 – 16 February 1969 | MONKEY | EARTH
17 February 1969 – 5 February 1970 | ROOSTER | EARTH

The 1970s

6 February 1970 – 26 January 1971 | DOG | METAL
27 January 1971 – 14 February 1972 | PIG | METAL
15 February 1972 – 2 February 1973 | RAT | WATER
3 February 1973 – 22 January 1974 | OX | WATER
23 January 1974 – 10 February 1975 | TIGER | WOOD
11 February 1975 – 30 January 1976 | RABBIT | WOOD
31 January 1976 – 17 February 1977 | DRAGON | FIRE
18 February 1977 – 6 February 1978 | SNAKE | FIRE
7 February 1978 – 27 January 1979 | HORSE | EARTH
28 January 1979 – 15 February 1980 | GOAT | EARTH

The 1980s

16 February 1980 – 4 February 1981 | MONKEY | METAL
5 February 1981 – 24 January 1982 | ROOSTER | METAL
25 January 1982 – 12 February 1983 | DOG | WATER
13 February 1983 – 1 February 1984 | PIG | WATER
2 February 1984 – 19 February 1985 | RAT | WOOD
20 February 1985 – 8 February 1986 | OX | WOOD
9 February 1986 – 28 January 1987 | TIGER | FIRE
29 January 1987 – 16 February 1988 | RABBIT | FIRE
17 February 1988 – 5 February 1989 | DRAGON | EARTH
6 February 1989 – 26 January 1990 | SNAKE | EARTH

The 1990s

27 January 1990 – 14 February 1991 | HORSE | METAL
15 February 1991 – 3 February 1992 | GOAT | METAL
4 February 1992 – 22 January 1993 | MONKEY | WATER

23 January 1993 – 9 February 1994 | ROOSTER | WATER
10 February 1994 – 30 January 1995 | DOG | WOOD
31 January 1995 – 18 February 1996 | PIG | WOOD
19 February 1996 – 7 February 1997 | RAT | FIRE
8 February 1997 – 27 January 1998 | OX | FIRE
28 January 1998 – 5 February 1999 | TIGER | EARTH
6 February 1999 – 4 February 2000 | RABBIT | EARTH

The 2000s

5 February 2000 – 23 January 2001 | DRAGON | METAL
24 January 2001 – 11 February 2002 | SNAKE | METAL
12 February 2002 – 31 January 2003 | HORSE | WATER
1 February 2003 – 21 January 2004 | GOAT | WATER
22 January 2004 – 8 February 2005 | MONKEY | WOOD
9 February 2005 – 28 January 2006 | ROOSTER | WOOD
29 January 2006 – 17 February 2007 | DOG | FIRE
18 February 2007 – 6 February 2008 | PIG | FIRE
7 February 2008 – 25 January 2009 | RAT | EARTH
26 January 2009 – 13 February 2010 | OX | EARTH

The 2010s

14 February 2010 – 2 February 2011 | TIGER | METAL
3 February 2011 – 22 January 2012 | RABBIT | METAL
23 January 2012 – 9 February 2013 | DRAGON | WATER
10 February 2013 – 30 January 2014 | SNAKE | WATER
31 January 2014 – 18 February 2015 | HORSE | WOOD
19 February 2015 – 7 February 2016 | GOAT | WOOD
8 February 2016 – 27 January 2017 | MONKEY | FIRE
28 January 2017 – 15 February 2018 | ROOSTER | FIRE
16 February 2018 – 4 February 2019 | DOG | EARTH
5 February 2019 – 24 January 2020 | PIG | EARTH

The 2020s

25 January 2020 – 11 February 2021 | RAT | METAL
12 February 2021 – 1 February 2022 | OX | METAL
2 February 2022 – 21 January 2023 | TIGER | WATER

22 January 2023 – 9 February 2024 | RABBIT | WATER
10 February 2024 – 28 January 2025 | DRAGON | WOOD
29 January 2025 – 16 February 2026 | SNAKE | WOOD
17 February 2026 – 5 February 2027 | HORSE | FIRE
6 February 2027 – 25 January 2028 | GOAT | FIRE
26 January 2028 – 12 February 2029 | MONKEY | EARTH
13 February 2029 – 2 February 2030 | ROOSTER | EARTH

You may have noticed that the 'natural' basic element of your sign is not necessarily the same as the element of the year you were born. Don't worry about this. The element of your birth year takes precedence, though you could also read the qualities assigned to the natural element as well, as these will be relevant to your personality but to a lesser degree.

Metal

Metal is the element associated in China with gold and wealth. So, if you are a Metal child, you will be very good at accumulating money. The Metal individual is ambitious, even if their animal sign is not particularly career-minded. The Metal-born version of an unworldly sign will still somehow have an eye for a bargain or a good investment; they'll manage to buy at the right time when prices are low and be moved to sell just as the price is peaking. If they want to get rid of unwanted items, they'll potter along to a car boot sale and without appearing to try, somehow make a killing, selling the lot while stalls around them struggle for attention. Career-minded signs with the element Metal have to be careful they don't overdo things. They have a tendency to become workaholics. Wealth will certainly flow, but it could be at the expense of family harmony and social life.

The element of Metal adds power, drive, and tenacity to whatever sign it influences so if you were born in a Metal year, you'll never lack cash for long.

Water

Water is the element associated with communication, creativity, and the emotions. Water has a knack of flowing around obstacles, finding routes that are not obvious to the naked eye and seeping into the smallest cracks. So, if you're a Water child, you'll be very good at getting what you want in an oblique, unchallenging way. You are one of nature's lateral thinkers. You are also wonderful with people. You're sympathetic, empathetic, and can always find the right words at the right time. You can also be highly persuasive, but in such a subtle way nobody notices your influence or input. They think the whole thing was their own idea.

People born in Water years are very creative and extremely intuitive. They don't know where their inspiration comes from, but somehow ideas just pour into their brains. Many artists were born in Water years.

Animal signs that are normally regarded as a little impatient and tactless have their rough edges smoothed when they appear in a Water year. People born in these years will be more diplomatic, artistic, and amiable than other versions of their fellow signs. And if you were born in a naturally sensitive, emotional sign, in a Water year, you'll be so intuitive you're probably psychic. Yet just as water can fall as gentle nurturing rain, or a raging destructive flood, so Water types need to take care not to let their emotions run away with them or to allow themselves to use their persuasive skills to be too manipulative.

Wood

Wood is the element associated with growth and expansion. In Chinese astrology, Wood doesn't primarily refer to the inert variety used to make floorboards and furniture, it represents living, flourishing trees and smaller plants, all pushing out of the earth and growing towards the sky.

Wood is represented by the colour green, not brown. If you're a Wood child, you're likely to be honest, generous, and friendly. You think BIG and like to be involved in numerous projects, often at the same time.

Wood people are practical yet imaginative and able to enlist the support of others simply by the sincerity and enthusiasm with which they tackle their plans. Yet even though they're always busy with a project, they somehow radiate calm, stability, and confidence. There's a sense of the timeless serenity of a big old tree about Wood people. Other signs instinctively trust them and look to them for guidance.

Animal signs that could be prone to nervousness or impulsive behaviour tend to be calmer and more productive in Wood year versions, while signs whose natural element is also Wood could well end up leaders of vast teams or business empires. Wood people tend to sail smoothly through life, but they must guard against becoming either stubborn or unyielding as they grow older or alternatively, saying 'yes' to every new plan and overextending themselves.

Fire

Fire is the element associated with dynamism, strength, and persistence. Fire demands action, movement, and expansion. It also creates a huge amount of heat. Fire is precious when it warms our homes and cooks our food, and it possesses a savage beauty that's endlessly fascinating. Yet it's also highly dangerous and destructive if it gets out of control. Something of this ambivalent quality is evident in Fire children.

People born in Fire years tend to be immensely attractive, magnetic types. Other signs are drawn to them. Yet there is always a hint of danger, of unpredictability, about them. You never know quite where you are with a Fire year sign and in a way, this is part of their fascination.

People born in Fire years like to get things done. They are extroverted and bold and impatient for action. They are brilliant at getting things started and energising people and projects. Quieter signs born in a Fire year are more dynamic, outspoken, and energetic than their fellow sign cousins, while extrovert signs positively blaze with exuberance and confidence when Fire is added to the mix.

People born in Fire years will always be noticed, but they should try to remember they tend to be impatient and impulsive. Develop a habit of pausing to take a deep breath to consider things, before rushing in, and you won't get burned.

Earth

Earth is the element associated with patience, stability, and practicality. This may not sound exciting but, in Chinese astrology, Earth is at the centre of everything: the heart of the planet. Earth year children are strong, hardworking personalities. They will persist with a task if it's worthwhile and never give up until it's complete. They create structure and balance, and they have very nurturing instincts.

Women born in Earth years make wonderful mothers, and if they're not mothering actual children, they'll be mothering their colleagues at work, or their friends and relatives, while also filling their homes with houseplants and raising vegetables in the garden if at all possible.

Other signs like being around Earth types as they exude a sense of security. Earth people don't like change, and they strive to keep their lives settled and harmonious. They are deeply kind and caring and immensely honest. Tact is not one of their strong points, however. They will always say what they think, so if you don't want the unvarnished truth, better not to ask!

Earth lends patience and stability to the more flighty, over-emotional signs, and rock-solid integrity to the others. Earth people will be sought-after in whatever field they choose to enter, but they must take care not to become too stubborn. Make a point of seeking out and listening to a wide range of varying opinions before setting a decision in stone.

Yin and Yang

As you looked down the table of years and elements, you may have noticed that the elements came in pairs. Each element was repeated the following year. If the Monkey was Water one year, it would be followed immediately the next year by the Rooster, also Water.

This is because of Yin and Yang – the mysterious but vital forces that, in Chinese philosophy, are believed to control the planet and probably the whole universe. They can be thought of as positive and negative, light and dark, masculine and feminine, night and day, etc. but the important point is that everything is either Yin or Yang; the two forces complement each other and both are equally important because only together do they make up the whole. For peace and harmony to be achieved, both forces need to be in balance.

Each of the animal signs is believed to be either Yin or Yang and because of the need for balance and harmony, they alternate through the years. Six of the 12 signs are Yin and six are Yang and since Yang represents extrovert, dominant energy, the Yang sign is first, followed by the Yin sign which represents quiet, passive force. A Yang sign is always followed by a Yin sign throughout the cycle.

The Yang signs are:

Rat

Tiger

Dragon

Horse

Monkey

Dog

The Yin Signs are

Ox

Rabbit

Snake

Goat

Rooster

Pig

Although Yang is seen as a masculine energy, and Yin a feminine energy, in reality, whether you are male or female, everyone has a mixture of Yin and Yang within them. If you need to know, quickly, whether your sign is Yin or Yang just check your birth year. If it ends in an even number (or 0) your sign is Yang. If it ends in an odd number, your sign is Yin. (The only exception is if you're born in late January or early February and according to Chinese astrology you belong to the year before).

In general, Yang signs tend to be extrovert, action-oriented types while Yin signs are gentler, more thoughtful, and patient.

So, as balance is essential when an element controls a period of time, it needs to express itself in its stronger Yang form in a Yang year as well as in its gentler Yin form in a Yin year, to be complete.

This year of the Crimson Horse begins an exciting new two-year round, this time of the Fire element. A new element always arrives in its strong Yang form, so now (at the close of the Wood element in its quieter Yin form, brought in by the Snake), we get to experience a blast of the fiery new energy galloped in by the Horse, a bold Yang sign.

Next year, the second year of the Fire element will begin – this time in its gentler, Yin form trotted in by the amiable Goat. Think candle flame, as opposed to forest fire.

This cycle of elements always follows in exactly the same order. When the Fire element is complete, there will be two Earth years, then two Metal years, followed by two Water years and two Wood years, until finally – in 2036 and 2037 – two Fire years come around again. In 2036, Fire arrives courtesy of the Yang Fire Dragon and in 2037 the quieter Yin Fire Snake completes the duet.

But why do elements have Yin and Yang forms you might be wondering. It's to take into account the way elements can express themselves in strikingly different strengths. A candle flame and a raging inferno are both clearly forms of Fire, yet vary enormously in intensity. In the same way, a great oak tree and a blade of grass – both belong to the Wood element but at a vastly different scale.

For perfect harmony, Chinese wisdom asserts that each has to have its equal turn to be expressed. You can't have one without the other.

So, in Yang years, the influence of the ruling element will be strong and obvious. In Yin years, the qualities of the same element are still there, but playing out more quietly, like cosmic background music.

Friendly Elements

Just as some signs get on well together and others don't, so some elements work well together while others don't. These are the elements that exist in harmony:

METAL likes EARTH and WATER

WATER likes METAL and WOOD

WOOD likes WATER and FIRE

FIRE likes WOOD and EARTH

EARTH likes FIRE and METAL

The reason for these friendly partnerships is believed to be the natural, productive cycle. Water nourishes Wood and makes plants grow, Wood provides fuel for Fire, Fire produces ash which is a type of Earth, Earth can be melted or mined to produce Metal while Metal contains or carries Water in a bucket.

So, Water supports Wood, Wood supports Fire, Fire supports Earth, Earth supports Metal and Metal supports Water.

Unfriendly Elements

But since everything has to be in balance, all the friendly elements are opposed by the same number of unfriendly elements. These are the elements that are not in harmony:

METAL dislikes WOOD and FIRE

WATER dislikes FIRE and EARTH

WOOD dislikes EARTH and METAL

FIRE dislikes METAL and WATER

EARTH dislikes WOOD and WATER

The reason some elements don't get on, is down to the destructive cycle which is: Water puts out Fire and is absorbed by Earth, Wood breaks up Earth (with its strong roots) and is harmed by Metal tools, Metal is melted by Fire and can cut down Wood.

So, if someone just seems to rub you up the wrong way, for no logical reason, it could be that your elements clash.

CHAPTER 16: WESTERN HOROSCOPES AND CHINESE HOROSCOPES – THE LINK

So now, hopefully, you'll have all the tools you need to create your very own, personal, multi-faceted Chinese horoscope. But does that mean the Western-style astrological sign that you're more familiar with is no longer relevant?

Not necessarily. Purists may not agree, but the odd thing is there does seem to be an overlap between a person's Western birth sign and their Chinese birth month sign; the two together can add yet another interesting layer to the basic birth year personality.

A Rabbit born under the Western sign of Leo may turn out to be very different on the surface, to a Rabbit born under the Western sign of Pisces for instance.

Of course, Chinese astrology already takes this into account by including the season of birth in a full chart, but we can possibly refine the system even further by adding the characteristics we've learned from our Western Sun Signs into the jigsaw.

If you'd like to put this theory to the test, simply find your Chinese year sign and then look up your Western Astrological sign within it, from the list below. While you're at it, why not check out the readings for your partner and friends too? You could be amazed at how accurate the results turn out to be.

Horse

Aries Horse

Overflowing with energy the Aries Horse just can't sit still for long. These types just have to find an outlet for their phenomenal vitality. They are hardworking, hard-playing, and usually highly popular. Less fun-loving signs might be accused of being workaholics but not the Aries Horse. People born under this sign devote enormous amounts of time to their careers but still have so much spare capacity there is plenty left over for their friends. They always do well in their chosen profession.

Taurus Horse

The Taurus Horse can be a trickier creature. Charming yet logical, he has a very good brain and is not afraid to use it. The only problem is that without warning the Taurus Horse can turn from flighty and fun to immensely stubborn and even an earthquake wouldn't shift him from an entrenched position. Yet treated with understanding and patience, the Taurus Horse can be coaxed to produce wonderful achievements.

Gemini Horse

Gemini types are easily bored, and when they are born in the freedom-loving year of the Horse, this trait tends to be accentuated. Unless their attention is caught and held almost instantly, Gemini Horse subjects kick up their heels and gallop off to find more fun elsewhere. For this reason, they often find it difficult to hold on to a job, and they change careers frequently. Yet once they discover a subject about which they can feel passionate, they employ the whole of their considerable talent and will zoom to the top in record time.

Cancer Horse

The Cancer Horse is a lovable creature with a great many friends. These types tend to lack confidence and need a lot of praise and nurturing, but with the right leadership, they will move mountains. Some signs find them difficult to understand because the Cancer Horse loves to be surrounded by a crowd yet needs a lot of alone time too. Misjudge the mood, and the Cancer Horse can seem bafflingly unfriendly. Yet, stay the course, and these subjects become wonderfully loyal friends.

Leo Horse

People born under the star sign of Leo will be the first to admit they like to show off and when they are also born in the year of the Horse, they enjoy showing off all the more. These types love nothing better than strutting around rocking designer outfits while others look on in admiration. They are not so interested in home decor; it's their own personal appearance which counts most. The Leo Horse would much rather invest time and money boosting their image than shoving their earnings into a bank account to gather dust.

Virgo Horse

Virgo types can be a little solemn and over-devoted to duty, but when they are born in the year of the Horse, they are endowed with a welcome streak of equine frivolity. The Virgo Horse loves to party. He will make sure his work is completed first of course, but once the office door clicks shut behind him, the Virgo Horse really knows how to let his hair down.

Libra Horse

The Libra Horse is another true charmer. Friends and acquaintances by the score fill the address books of these types, and their diaries are crammed with appointments. Honest, trustworthy and helpful, other people can't help gravitating to them. Oddly enough, despite their gregarious nature, these types are also very independent. Sometimes too independent for their own good. They are excellent at giving advice to others but find it almost impossible to take advice themselves.

Scorpio Horse

The Scorpio Horse is a real thrill seeker. These types enjoy life's pleasures, particularly passionate pleasures and go all out to attain them. There is no middle road with the Scorpio Horse. These are all or nothing types. They fling themselves into the project of the moment wholeheartedly or not at all. They tend to see things in black and white and believe others are either for them or against them. In serious moments, the Scorpio Horse subscribes to some surprising conspiracy theories, but mostly they keep these ideas to themselves.

Sagittarius Horse

The star sign of Sagittarius is the sign of the Centaur – half-man half-horse – and when these types are born in the year of the Horse, the equine tendencies are so strong they practically have four hooves. Carefree country-lovers these subjects can't bear to be penned in and never feel totally happy until they are out of doors in some wide-open space. They crave fresh air and regular exercise and do best in joint activities. As long as they can spend enough time out of doors, Sagittarius Horses are blessed with glowing good health.

Capricorn Horse

The Capricorn Horse is a canny beast. These types are great savers. They manage to have fun on a shoestring and stash away every spare penny at the same time. They are prepared to work immensely hard provided the pay is good, and they have a remarkable knack of finding just the right job to make the most of their earning power. The Capricorn Horse likes a good time, and he will never be poor.

Aquarius Horse

When Aquarius meets the Horse, it results in a very curious creature. These types admit to enquiring minds; other less charitable signs might call them nosey parkers. Call them what you may, subjects born under this sign need to know and discover. They often become inventors, and they have a weakness for new gadgets and the latest technology. The Aquarius Horse can be wildly impractical and annoy partners by frittering cash away on their latest obsession. They also tend to fill their living space with peculiar objects from junk shops and car boot sales, which they intend to upcycle into useful treasures. Somehow, they seldom get round to finishing the project.

Pisces Horse

Artistic Pisces adds an unusual dimension to the physical Horse, who normally has little time for cultural frills and foibles. These types are great home entertainers and often gifted cooks as well. They invite a group of friends around at the slightest excuse and can conjure delicious snacks and drinks from the most unpromising larders. They adore company and get melancholy if left alone too long.

Goat

Aries Goat

Normally mild and unassuming, the Goat can become almost argumentative when born under the star sign of Aries. Though friendly and very seldom cross, the Aries Goat will suddenly adopt an unexpectedly stubborn position and stick to it unreasonably even when it's obvious he is wrong. Despite this, these types are blessed with sunny natures and are quickly forgiven. They don't bear a grudge and have no idea – after the awkwardness – that anything unpleasant occurred.

Taurus Goat

Like his Aries cousin, the Taurus Goat can turn stubborn too. These types have a very long fuse. Most people would assume they did not have a temper because it is so rarely displayed. But make them truly angry, and they will explode. Small they may be, but a raging Goat can be a fearful sight. On the other hand, these Goats are more likely to have a sweet tooth than their cousins, so if you do upset them, a choccy treat could work wonders in making amends.

Gemini Goat

The Goat born under Gemini is a terrible worrier. These types seem to use their active minds to dream up all the troubles and problems that could result from every single action. Naturally, this renders decision-making almost impossible. They dither and rethink and ponder until finally someone else makes up their mind for them, at which point they are quite happy. In fact, if the Gemini Goat never had to make another decision, she would be a blissfully content creature.

Cancer Goat

Gentle, soft-hearted and kind, the Cancer Goat is a friend to all in need. These types would give their last penny to a homeless beggar in the street, and they always have a shoulder ready should anyone need to cry on it. Yet they can also be surprisingly moody for what appears to be no reason at all, and this characteristic can be baffling to their friends. No point in wasting time asking what's wrong, they find it difficult to explain. Just wait for the clouds to pass.

Leo Goat

The Leo Goat is a very fine specimen. Warm, friendly and more extrovert than her quieter Goat cousins, she seems to have the confidence other Goats often lack. Look more closely though, and you can find all is not quite as it seems. Frequently, that self-assured appearance is merely a well-presented 'front'. Back in the privacy of their own home, the bold Leo Goat can crumble. In truth, these types are easily hurt.

Virgo Goat

Outwardly vague and preoccupied, the Virgo Goat can turn unexpectedly fussy. These types are easy-going, but they can't stand messy homes, mud in their car or sweet wrappers lying around. Yet they would be genuinely surprised if anyone accused them of being pernickety. They believe they are laid back and good-humoured, which they are. Just don't drop chewing gum on their front path, that's all, and take your shoes off at the door.

Libra Goat

The Libra Goat is obliging to the point of self-sacrifice. These types are truly nice people. Generous with their time as well as their possessions. Unfortunately, their good nature is sometimes exploited by the unscrupulous. The Libra Goat will wear itself out in the service of those in distress, will refuse to hear a bad word about anyone and will remain loyal to friends despite the most intense provocation. The Libra Goat lives to please.

Scorpio Goat

Scorpio Goats are among the most strong-willed of all the Goats. They like to go their own way and hate to have others tell them what to do. They don't mind leaving irksome chores and duties to others, but woe betides anyone who tries to interfere with the Scorpio Goat's pet project. At first sight, they may appear preoccupied and have their heads in the clouds, but beneath that vague exterior, their sharp eyes miss very little. Don't underestimate the Scorpio Goat.

Sagittarius Goat

Sagittarius lends an adventurous streak to the normally cautious Goat make-up, and these types tend to take far more risks than their cousins born at other times of the year. While they still enjoy being taken care of, the Sagittarius Goat prefers cosseting on his return from adventures, not instead of them. These types are often good in business and amaze everyone by doing 'extremely well' apparently by accident.

Capricorn Goat

The Capricorn Goat, in contrast, is a very cautious creature. Danger beckons at every turn and security is top of their list of priorities. This Goat can never get to sleep until every door and window has been locked and secured. Should they find themselves staying in a hotel, Capricorn Goats will often drag a chair in front of the bedroom door, just in case. These types are difficult to get to know because it takes a while to win their trust, but once they become friends, they will be loyal forever and despite their caution – or sensible outlook as they'd call it – they can be very successful.

Aquarius Goat

The Aquarius Goat tends to leap about from one high-minded project to the next. These well-meaning types might be manning a soup kitchen one day and devising a scheme to combat climate change the next. Their grand plans seldom come to fruition because they find the practical details so difficult to put into operation but should they link up with an organisational genius they could achieve great things.

Pisces Goat

The Pisces Goat is a very sensitive soul. These types are often highly gifted, and their best course of action is to find someone to take care of them as soon as possible so that they can get on with cultivating their talents. Left to themselves Pisces Goats will neglect their physical needs, failing to cook proper meals or dress warmly in cold weather. With the right guidance, however, they can work wonders.

Monkey

Aries Monkey

These cheeky types have a charm that is quite irresistible. Energetic and mischievous they adore parties and social gatherings of any kind. They crop up on every guest list because they are so entertaining. The Aries Monkey is a font of funny stories and silly jokes but seldom stands still for long. Friends of the Aries Monkey are often frustrated as their popular companion is so in demand it's difficult to pin her down for a catch-up.

Taurus Monkey

The Monkey born under the star sign of Taurus has a little more weight in his character. These types take life a shade more seriously than their delightfully frivolous cousins. Not that the Taurus Monkey is ever a stick-in-the-mud. It's just that business comes before pleasure with these types, although only just, and the business that catches their eye is not necessarily what others would call business. Taurus Monkey is as captivated by creating a useful container out of an old coffee jar as checking out a balance sheet.

Gemini Monkey

The Gemini Monkey Is a true comedian. Incredibly quick-witted, these types only have to open their mouths, and everyone around them is in stitches. If Oscar Wilde was not a Gemini Monkey, he should have been. People born under this sign could easily make a career in the comedy field if they can be bothered to make enough attempts. Truth is they're just as happy entertaining their friends as a theatre full of people.

Cancer Monkey

These types have a gentler side to their characters. Cancer Monkey's love to tinker with machinery and see how things work. They tend to take things to pieces and then forget to put them together again. They are easily hurt, however, if someone complains about this trait. They genuinely intend to put things right. It is just that, somehow, they never manage to get round to it, and they never realise that this is a trait they repeat over and over again.

Leo Monkey

The Leo Monkey is a highly adaptable creature. He can be all things to all men while still retaining his own unique personality. Popular, amusing and fond of practical jokes these types are welcome wherever they go. They can sometimes get rather carried away with the sound of their own voices and end up being rather tactless, but such is their charm that everyone forgives them. Occasionally, a practical joke can go too far, but kind-hearted Leo Monkey is horrified if anyone feels hurt, and instantly apologises.

Virgo Monkey

The Virgo Monkey could be a great inventor. The Monkey's natural ingenuity blends with Virgo's patience and fussiness over detail to create a character with the ideas to discover something new and the tenacity to carry on until it is perfected. If they could curb their impulse to rush on to the next brilliant idea when the last is complete, and turned their intention instead to marketing, they could make a fortune.

Libra Monkey

The Monkey born under the sign of Libra is actually a force to be reckoned with though no-one would ever guess it. These types are lovable and fun and have a knack of getting other people to do what they want without even realising they've been talked into it. In fact, Libran Monkeys are first-class manipulators but so skilled at their craft that nobody minds. These types could get away with murder.

Scorpio Monkey

Normally, the Monkey is a real chatterbox, but when Scorpio is added to the mix, you have a primate with the unusual gift of discretion right alongside his natural loquaciousness. These types will happily gossip all day long, but if they need to keep a secret, they are able to do so, to the grave if necessary. Scorpio Monkey could be an actor or a spy – and play each role to perfection. 007 could well have been a Scorpio Monkey.

Sagittarius Monkey

These flexible, amorous, adventure-loving Monkeys add zing to any gathering. These are the guests with the mad-cap ideas who want to jump fully clothed into the swimming pool at midnight and think it terrific fun to see in the New Year on top of Ben Nevis. It's difficult to keep up with the Sagittarius Monkey, but it's certainly fun to try.

Capricorn Monkey

Capricorn Monkeys have their serious side, but they are also flirty types. These are the subjects who charm with ease and tease and joke their conquests into bed. The trouble is Capricorn Monkey often promises more than is deliverable. These types tire more easily than they realise, and can't always put their exciting schemes into action. This rarely stops them trying, of course.

Aquarius Monkey

The Aquarius Monkey is a particularly inventive creature and employs his considerable intellect in trying to discover new ways to save the world. These types often have a hard time in their early years as it takes them decades to realise that not everyone sees the importance of their passions as they do. But, once they understand a different approach is needed, they go on to accomplish much in later life.

Pisces Monkey

The Pisces Monkey can be a puzzling creature. These types are dreamy and amusing one minute and irritable and quick-tempered the next. They can go with the flow so far and then suddenly wonder why no-one can keep up with them when they decide to get a move on. They tend to lack quite so much humour when the joke is on themselves, but most of the time they are agreeable companions.

Rooster

Aries Rooster

Stand well back when confronted with an Aries Rooster. These types are one hundred percent go-getter, and nothing will stand in their way. Aries Rooster can excel at anything to which he puts his mind, and as he frequently puts his mind to business matters, he's likely to end up a billionaire. Think scarlet sports cars, ostentatious homes, and a personal helicopter or two – the owner is bound to be an Aries Rooster.

Taurus Rooster

The Taurus Rooster has a heart of gold but can come over as a bit of a bossy boots, particularly in financial matters. These types believe they have a unique understanding of money and accounts and are forever trying to get more sloppy signs to sharpen up in this department. Even if their manner rankles, it's worth listening to their advice. Annoyingly, they are often right.

Gemini Rooster

The Rooster born under the sign of Gemini would make a terrific private detective were it not for the fact that Roosters find it almost impossible to blend into the background. Gemini Roosters love to find out what's going on and have an uncanny ability to stumble on the one thing you don't wish them to know. They mean no harm, however, and once they find a suitable outlet for their talents, they will go far.

Cancer Rooster

The Rooster born under the sign of Cancer is often a fine-looking creature and knows it. These types are secretly rather vain and behind the scenes take great pains with their appearance. They would die rather than admit it, however, and like to give the impression that their wonderful style is no more than a happy accident. Though they cultivate a relaxed, easy-going manner, a bad hair day or a splash of mud on their new suede boots is enough to send them into a major sulk for hours.

Leo Rooster

Not everyone takes to the Leo Rooster. The Lion is a naturally proud, extrovert sign and when allied to the strutting Rooster, there is a danger of these types ending up as bossy exhibitionists. Yet they really have the kindest of hearts and will leap from their pedestals in an instant to comfort someone who seems upset. A word of warning – they should avoid excessive alcohol as these types can get merry on a sniff of a cider apple.

Virgo Rooster

The Virgo Rooster is a hardworking, dedicated creature, devoted to family, but in an undemonstrative way. Wind this bird up at your peril, however. These types have little sense of humour when it comes to taking a joke, and they will hold a grudge for months if they feel someone has made them look foolish. They hate to be laughed at.

Libra Rooster

The Libra Rooster likes to look good, have a fine home and share his considerable assets with his closest friends. These types enjoy admiration, but they are more subtle than Leo Roosters and don't demand it quite so openly. Libra Rooster is quite happy to give but does expect gratitude in return.

Scorpio Rooster

The Scorpio Rooster is a heroic creature. These types will defend a position to the death. In days of old, many a Scorpio Rooster will have got involved in a duel because these types cannot endure insults, will fight aggression with aggression and will not back down under any circumstances. Foolhardy they may appear, but there is something admirable about them nevertheless.

Sagittarius Rooster

The Sagittarius Rooster tends to be a little excitable and rash. These types are bold and brash and ready for anything. They love to travel and are desperate to see what's over the next hill and around the next bend. Born explorers' they never want to tread the conventional travel path. Let others holiday in Marbella if they wish. Sagittarius Rooster prefers a walking tour of Tibet.

Capricorn Rooster

Capricorn brings a steadying quality to the impulsive Rooster. These types like to achieve, consolidate, and then build again. They believe they are amassing a fortune for their family and they usually do. However, sometimes, their families would prefer a little less security and more attention. Best not to mention it to Capricorn Rooster though – this Rooster is likely to feel hurt and offended.

Aquarius Rooster

The Aquarius Rooster is frequently misunderstood. These types mean well but they tend to be impulsive and speak before they think, accidentally offending others when they do so. In fact, the Aquarius Rooster is a sensitive creature beneath that brash exterior and is easily hurt. If they can learn to count to ten before saying anything controversial, and maybe rephrase, they'd be amazed at how successful they'd become.

Pisces Rooster

The Pisces Rooster has a secret fear. He is terrified that one day he will be terribly poor. These types save hard to stave off that dreadful fate and will only feel totally relaxed when they have a huge nest egg behind them. Despite this, they manage to fall in and out of love regularly and often end up delighting their partners with the wonderful lifestyle they can create.

Dog

Aries Dog

The Aries Dog is a friendly type. Extrovert and sociable these subjects like a lively career and cheerful home life. They are not excessively materialistic, but they tend to make headway in the world without trying too hard. Aries Dog likes to get things done and will bound from one task to the next with energy and enthusiasm.

Taurus Dog

The Dog born under the star sign of Taurus is the most dependable creature in the world. Their word really is their bond, and they will never break a promise while there is breath in their body. They tend to be ultra-conservative with a small 'c'. The men are inclined to be chauvinists, and the women usually hold traditional views. They really do prefer to make their home and family their priority. They are loyal and kind, and people instinctively trust them.

Gemini Dog

The Gemini Dog, in contrast, while never actually dishonest, can be a bit of a sly fox when necessary. The quickest of all Dogs, the Gemini breed gets impatient when the going gets slow and resorts to the odd trick to speed things along. Nevertheless, these types are truthful and honest in their own way and have a knack of falling on their feet… whatever happens.

Cancer Dog

The Cancer Dog was born to be in a settled relationship. These types are never totally happy until they've found their true love and built a cosy home to snuggle up in together. Cancer Dog is not overly concerned with a career. As long as these types earn enough to pay the mortgage and buy life's essentials, they are happy. The right companionship is what they crave. With the perfect partner by their side, they are truly content.

Leo Dog

If Leo Dogs really did have four legs, chances are they would be police dogs. These types are sticklers for law and order. They will not tolerate injustice and will seek out wrongdoers and plague them until they change their ways. Woe betide any workmate who is pilfering pens, making free with office coffee or fiddling expenses. The Leo Dog will force them to own up and make amends. Should you be a victim of injustice, however, Leo Dog will zoom to your aid.

Virgo Dog

The Virgo Dog tends to be a great worrier. A born perfectionist, Virgo Dog agonises over every detail and loses sleep if he suspects he has performed any task badly. These types are very clever and can achieve great things, but too often they fail to enjoy their success because they are too busy worrying they might have made a mistake. The crazy thing is, they very seldom do.

Libra Dog

The Libra Dog believes in 'live and let live'. A laid back, tolerant fellow, Libra Dog likes to lie in the sun and not interfere with anyone. Let sleeping dogs lie is definitely her motto. She will agree to almost anything for a quiet life. Yet it's unwise to push her too far. When there's no alternative, this particular hound can produce a very loud bark.

Scorpio Dog

The Scorpio Dog is as loyal and trustworthy as other canines, but more difficult to get to know. Beneath that amiable exterior is a very suspicious heart. These types don't quite understand why they are so wary of others, but it takes them a long time to learn to trust. Perhaps they are afraid of getting hurt. The idea of marriage fills them with terror, and it takes a very patient partner to get them to the altar. Once married, however, they will be faithful and true.

Sagittarius Dog

The Sagittarius Dog is inexhaustible. These cheerful types are always raring to go and quite happy to join in with any adventure. They love to be part of the gang and are perfectly willing to follow someone else's lead. They don't mind if their ideas are not always accepted; they just like being involved. These types work splendidly in teams and can achieve great things in a group.

Capricorn Dog

The Capricorn Dog is a very caring type. These subjects are happy so long as their loved ones are happy, but they greatly fear that a friend or family member might fall ill. This concern, probably kept secret, gives them real anxiety and should a loved one show worrying symptoms, the Capricorn Dog will suffer sleepless nights until the problem is resolved. When they are not urging their families to keep warm and put on an extra vest, these types are likely to be out and about helping others less fortunate than themselves.

Aquarius Dog

The Aquarius Dog, when young, spends a great deal of time searching for a worthy cause to which they can become devoted. Since there are so many worthy causes from which to choose these types can suffer much heartache as they struggle to pick the right one. When – at last – a niche is found, however, the Aquarius Dog will settle down to a truly contented life of quiet satisfaction. These types need to serve and feel that they are improving life for others. This is their path to happiness.

Pisces Dog

Like the Aquarius breed, the Pisces Dog often has a number of false starts early in life although these are more likely to be of a romantic rather than philanthropic nature. The Pisces Dog wants to find a soulmate but is not averse to exploring a few cul-de-sacs on the way.

These types are not promiscuous, however, and when they do find Mr or Miss Right, they are blissfully happy to settle down.

Pig

Aries Pig

The Aries Pig always seems to wear a smile on its face and no wonder. Everything seems to go right for these cheerful types, and they scarcely seem to have to lift a finger to make things fall perfectly into place. In fact, of course, their good luck is the result of sheer hard work, but the Aries Pig has a knack of making work look like play so that nobody realises the effort Pig is putting in.

Taurus Pig

Most Pigs are happy, but the Taurus Pigs really seem quite blissful most of the time. One of their favourite occupations is eating, and they delight in dreaming up sumptuous menus and then creating them for the enjoyment of themselves and their friends. For this reason, Taurus Pigs have a tendency to put on weight. Despite the time they devote to their hobby, however, Taurus Pigs usually do well in their career. Many gifted designers are born under this sign.

Gemini Pig

The Gemini Pig has a brilliant business brain gift-wrapped in a charming, happy go lucky personality. These types usually zoom straight to the top of their chosen tree, but they manage to do so smoothly and easily without ruffling too many feathers on the way. They are popular with their workmates, and later their employees, and nobody can figure out how quite such a nice, down to earth type has ended up in such a position of authority.

Cancer Pig

The Cancer Pig likes to give the impression of being a very hard-working type. She is hard working, of course, but perhaps not quite as excessively as she likes others to believe. Secretly, the Cancer Pig makes sure there's plenty of time to spare for fun and indulgence. To the outside world, however, Pig pretends to be constantly slaving away and likes to get regular appreciation for these efforts.

Leo Pig

The Leo Pig is delightful company. Friendly, amusing and very warm and approachable. These types do however have a tremendously lazy streak. Left to themselves, they would not rise till noon, and they prefer someone else to do all the cleaning and cooking. The Leo Pig has to be nagged to make an effort, but when these types do so, they can achieve impressive results.

Virgo Pig

The Virgo Pig, in contrast, is a highly conscientious creature. These types can't abide laziness, and while they are normally kindly, helpful souls who gladly assist others, they will not lift a finger to aid someone who has brought his problems on himself through slovenliness. The Virgo Pig is a clean, contented type who usually achieves a happy life.

Libra Pig

The creative Libra Pig is always dreaming up new ways to improve their home. These types love to be surrounded by beautiful and comfortable things but seldom get round to completing their ideas because they are having such a good time in other ways. This is probably just as well because the minute they decide on one colour scheme, they suddenly see something that might work better. A permanent work in progress is probably the best option.

Scorpio Pig

The Scorpio Pig usually goes far. The amiable Pig boosted by powerful, almost psychic Scorpio can seem turbo-charged at times. These types keep their own counsel more than their chatty cousins, and this often stands them in good stead in business. They can be a little too cautious at times, but they rarely make mistakes.

Sagittarius Pig

Eat, drink and be merry is the motto of the Sagittarius Pig. These types have the intelligence to go far in their careers but, in truth, they would rather party. They love to dress up, get together with a bunch of friends and laugh and dance until dawn. Sagittarius Pig hates to be alone for long, so is always off in search of company.

Capricorn Pig

Pigs are normally broad-minded types, but the Capricorn Pig is a little more staid than his cousins. Nevertheless, being able to narrow their vision gives these types the ability to channel their concentration totally onto the subject in hand, a gift which is vital to success in many professions. For this reason, Capricorn Pigs often make a name for themselves in their chosen career.

Aquarius Pig

Honest, straightforward and popular Aquarius Pigs have more friends than they can count. Always good-humoured and cheerful these types gravitate to those in need and do whatever they can to help. The Aquarius Pig gives copiously to charity and frequently wishes to do more. These types tend to have their heads in the clouds most of the time and for this reason, tend not to give their careers or finances the attention they should. But since worldly success means little to the Aquarius Pig, this hardly matters.

Pisces Pig

The Pisces Pig is a particularly sweet-natured creature. These types are real dreamers. They float around in a world of their own, and people tend to make allowances for them. Yet, from time to time, the Pisces Pig drifts in from his other planet to startle everyone with a stunningly brilliant idea. There is more to the Pisces Pig than meets the eye.

Rat

Aries Rat

Fiery Aries adds more than usual urgency to the sociable Rat. While these types enjoy company, they also tend to be impatient and can get quite bad-tempered and aggressive with anyone who seems to waste their time. Aries Rats do not suffer fools and will stomp off on their own if someone annoys them. In fact, this is the best thing all round. Aries Rats hate to admit it, but they benefit from a little solitude which enables them to calm down and recharge their batteries. Happily, as quickly as these types flare up, they just as quickly cool off again.

Taurus Rat

When Taurus, renowned for a love of luxury and the finer things in life, is born in a comfort-loving Rat year, a true gourmet and bon viveur has entered the world. The Taurus effect enhances the sensuous parts of the Rat personality and lifts them to new heights. Good food is absolutely essential to these types. They don't eat to live; they really do live to eat. Many excellent chefs are born under this sign, and even those folks who don't make catering their career are likely to be outstanding home cooks. Dinner parties thrown by Taurus Rats are memorable affairs. The only drawback with these types is that they can become a little pernickety and overly fussy about details. They also have to watch their weight.

Gemini Rat

While Taurus accentuates the Rat's love of good living, Gemini heightens the Rat's already well-developed social skills. That crowd chuckling and laughing around the witty type in the corner are bound to be listening to a Gemini Rat. Amusing, quick-thinking, and never lost for words, the only things likely to drive Gemini Rats away are bores and undue seriousness. Gemini Rats prefer light, entertaining conversation and head for the hills when things get too heavy. Delightful as they always are however, it is difficult to capture the attention of a Gemini Rat for long. These types love to circulate. They make an entrance and then move on to pastures new. Pinning them down never works. They simply lose interest and with it that famous sparkle.

Cancer Rat

Cancer makes the Rat a little more sensitive and easily hurt than usual. These types are emotional and loving but sometimes come across as martyrs. They work hard but tend to feel, often without good cause, their efforts are not as well appreciated as they should be. Cancer Rats frequently suspect they are being taken for granted at home and at work, but their love of company prevents them from making too big a fuss. Rats are naturally gifted business people, and the Cancer Rat has a particularly good head for financial affairs. These types enjoy working with others, and they are especially well suited to partnerships. However, don't expect the sensitive, feeling Cancer Rat to be a pushover. These types can be surprisingly demanding at work and will not tolerate any laziness on the part of employees.

Leo Rat

Leo Rats usually get to the top. Few people can resist them. The combination of Rat sociability, business acumen and ambition, coupled with extrovert Leo's rather, shall we say, 'pushy', qualities and flair for leadership can't help but power these types to the top of whatever tree they happen to choose to climb. Along the way, however, they may irritate those few less gifted souls who fail to fall under their spell. Such doubters may complain that Leo Rat hogs the limelight and tends to become overbearing at times but since hardly anyone else seems to notice, why should Leo Rat care?

Virgo Rat

As we have already seen, the delightful Rat does have a stingy streak in his make-up, and when the astrological sign of Virgo is added to the mix, this characteristic tends to widen. At best, Virgo Rats are terrific savers and do wonders with their investments. The Rat tendency to squander money on unwise bargains is almost entirely absent in these types, and they often end up seriously rich. At worst, however, in negative types, Virgo Rats can be real Scrooges, grating the last sliver of soap to save on washing powder, sitting in the dark to conserve electricity and attempting their own shoe repairs with stick-on soles, even when they have plenty of money in the bank. Virgo Rats are brilliant at detail; but in negative types, they put this gift to poor use spending far too long on money-saving schemes when they would do much better to look for ways of expanding their income.

Libra Rat

The Libra Rat adores company even more than most. In fact, these types are seldom alone. They have dozens of friends, their phones never stop ringing, and most evenings the Libra Rat is entertaining. Libra Rat enjoys civilised gatherings rather than wild parties and friends will be treated to beautiful music, exquisite food and a supremely comfortable home. These types really can charm the birds off the trees, not with the brilliant repartee of the Gemini Rat but with a warmth and low-key humour all their own. These types do tend to be a touch lazier than the usual Rat and their weakness for bargains, particularly in the areas of art and fashion, is more pronounced, but their charm is so strong that partners forgive them for overspending.

Scorpio Rat

It's often said that Rats would make good journalists or detectives because beneath that expansive surface is a highly observant brain. Well, the best of them all would be the Rat born under Scorpio. A veritable Sherlock Holmes of a Rat if you wish to be flattering, or a real nosey parker if you don't. These types are endlessly curious. They want to know everything that's going on, who is doing what with whom where and for how long. They may not have any particular use for the information they gather, but they just can't help gathering it all the same. Scorpio Rats often have psychic powers though they may not be aware of this and these powers aid them in their 'research'. Unlike other Rats, those born under Scorpio prefer their own company and like to work alone. When they manage to combine their curiosity and talent for digging out information, there is almost no limit to what they can achieve with their career

Sagittarius Rat

Traditionally Rats have many friends, but the Sagittarius Rat has the not so welcome distinction of collecting a few enemies along the way as well. The Sagittarius Rat finds this quite extraordinary as he never intends to upset anyone. It's just that these types can be forthright to the point of rudeness and an affable nature can only compensate so far. These types are amicable and warm, but when they speak their minds, some people never forgive them. Despite this tendency, Sagittarius Rats have a knack for accumulating money and plough it back into their business to good effect. They manage to be generous, and a bit mean at the same time, which baffles their friends, but those that have not been offended by Sagittarius Rat's tactless tongue tend to stay loyal forever.

Capricorn Rat

Rats are naturally high achievers, but perhaps the highest achiever of them all is likely to be born under the sign of Capricorn. These types are not loud and brilliant like Leo Rats. They tend to be quietly ambitious. They keep in the background, watching what needs to be done, astutely judging who counts and who does not, and then when they are absolutely sure they are on solid ground, they move in. After such preparation, they are unlikely to make a mistake, but if they do they blame themselves, they are bitterly angry, and they resolve never to repeat their stupidity. Reckless these types are not, but their methods produce good results, and they make steady progress towards their goals.

Aquarius Rat

All Rats are blessed with good brains, but few of them think of themselves as intellectuals. The exceptions are the Rats born under the sign of Aquarius. While being friendly and sociable, the Aquarian Rat also needs time alone to think things through and to study the latest subject that has aroused his interest. Perhaps not so adept at business as most Rats, those born under the sign of Aquarius make up for any deficiency in this department by teeming with good ideas. They are intuitive, very hard working and love to be involved in 'people' projects.

Pisces Rat

Pisces Rats tend to be quieter than their more flamboyant brothers and sisters. They are not drawn to the limelight, and they are not so interested in business as other Rats. In fact, working for other people has little appeal for them, although this is what they often end up doing through want of thinking up a better idea. Should a more enterprising Pisces Rat decide to put his mind to business, however, he will often end up self-employed which suits him extremely well. Having taken the plunge, many a self-employed Pisces Rat surprises himself by doing very well indeed. These types can be amazingly shrewd and intuitive, and once these powers are harnessed to the right career, they progress in leaps and bounds. Pisces Rats tend to do well in spite of themselves.

Ox

Aries Ox

Dynamic Aries brings the Ox a very welcome blast of fire and urgency to stir those methodical bones into faster action. This is a fortunate combination because when the steadfast, industrious, patient qualities of the Ox are combined with quickness of mind and a definite purpose, very little can stand in the way of this subject's progress. Aries Oxen do particularly well in careers where enormous discipline combined with flair and intelligence is required. Many writers are born under this sign as are college lecturers, historical researchers and archaeologists.

Taurus Ox

Oxen are notoriously stubborn creatures but combine them with Taurus the bull and this trait is doubled if not quadrupled. It is not a good idea to box these types into a corner because they will take a stand and refuse to budge even if the house is on fire. Taurean Oxen really will cut off their noses to spite their faces if they feel they have to. Fall out with them and stop talking, and the chances are that the feud will continue to the grave. Yet despite this tendency, Oxen born under the sign of Taurus are not unfriendly types. They are utterly reliable and totally loyal. Family and friends trust them completely. They might be a bit old fashioned and inflexible, but they are lovable too.

Gemini Ox

Chatty Gemini transforms the normally taciturn Ox into a beast which is almost loquacious, at least by the normal standards of these strong silent types. They might even be confident enough to attempt a few jokes, and though humour is not the Oxen's strongpoint, the Gemini Ox can usually produce something respectably amusing if not sidesplittingly funny. Oddly enough, should the Ox set his mind to it and apply his awesome hard work and patience to the subject of humour he might even make a career of it. Some Gemini Oxen have even become accomplished comedians – not simply through natural talent but through sheer hard work and perseverance. More frequently, however, the combination of Gemini with the Ox produces a 'poor man's lawyer' – a highly opinionated individual who can see what's wrong with the government and the legal system and loves to put the world to rights at every opportunity.

Cancer Ox

Oxen born under the sign of Cancer can go very far indeed, not through the application of brainpower although they are by no means unintelligent, but through the skills they have at their fingertips. These subjects are the craftsmen of the universe. Diligent, painstaking, and precise, they are incapable of bodging any practical task they undertake. They will spend hours and hours honing whatever craft has taken their fancy until they reach what looks to others like the peak of perfection. The Cancer Ox won't accept this of course. He can detect the minutest flaw in his own handiwork, but when he is finally forced to hand it over, everyone else is delighted with his efforts. Many artists, potters and sculptors are born under this sign.

Leo Ox

When the Lion of Leo meets the enormous strength of the Ox, the result is a formidable individual, indeed. Annoy or mock these powerful types at your peril. And anyone who dares to pick a fight with the Lion-Ox is likely to come out of it very badly. Most of the time, however, Leo is a friendly lion bringing confidence and a more relaxed attitude to the unbending Ox. These types are more broad-minded and open-hearted than the usual Oxen. They have been known to enjoy parties and once tempted into the limelight they may even find it's not as bad as they feared. In fact, secretly, they're having a ball.

Virgo Ox

Oxen born under the sign of Virgo tend to be very caring types. Though they show their feelings in practical ways and shun sloppy, emotional displays you can rely on an Ox born under Virgo to comfort the sick, help the old folk and notice if anyone in the neighbourhood needs assistance. Florence Nightingale could have been a Virgo Ox. The unsentimental but immensely useful and humane work she did for her sick soldiers is typical of these types. They make excellent nurses and care workers, forever plumping pillows, smoothing sheets and knowing just the right touches to bring comfort where it is needed. On a personal level, these subjects are inclined to be critical and easily irritated by the small failings of others, but their bark is worse than their bite. Their kindness shines through.

Libra Ox

Generally speaking, the down to earth Ox has little time for putting on the charm. As far as Ox is concerned, people either like you or they don't, and it's not worth worrying about it either way. There's no point in wasting valuable time trying to bend your personality to accommodate the whims of others. Yet when the Ox is born under the sign of Libra, this trait is modified somewhat. Libra people just can't help having charm even if they are Oxen and therefore express that charm more brusquely than usual. The Libran Ox glides effortlessly through life, pleasing others without even realising it. These types are sympathetic and like to help those in need wherever possible. Try to take advantage of their good nature or trick them with an untrue sob story, though, and they will never forgive you.

Scorpio Ox

The typical Ox is notoriously difficult to get to know, and when that Ox happens to be born under the secretive sign of Scorpio, you might as well give up and go home. You'll learn nothing from this creature unless he has some special reason for telling you. Stubborn and silent, these types are very deep indeed; they care nothing for the opinions of others and follow their own impenetrable hearts come what may. However, win the love of one of these unique subjects, and you have a very rare prize indeed. You will unlock a devotion and passion that you have probably never experienced before and will probably never experience again. This is a strangely compelling combination.

Sagittarius Ox

The Ox born under Sagittarius is a more carefree type than his brothers and sisters. Something of the free spirit of the horse touches these subjects, and while there is no chance of them kicking up their heels or doing anything remotely irresponsible, they at least understand these temptations in others and take a more relaxed view of life. The Ox born under Sagittarius is ambitious but independent. These types don't like to be told what to do and are probably more suited to being self-employed than working for others. They are more easy-going than a lot of Oxen and for this reason attract a wider range of friends. Like their Gemini cousins, they might even hazard a joke from time to time. All in all, the Ox born under Sagittarius gets more fun out of life.

Capricorn Ox

Unlike his Sagittarian brother, the Ox born under Capricorn takes himself and life very seriously indeed. These types usually do very well in material terms and often end up in positions of authority; yet if they're not careful, they can look burned out. With good reason. Capricorn Oxen have never learned how to relax, and they see life as a struggle; consequently, for them, it is. Yet they have much to be glad for. They are great savers for a rainy day, and so they never have to worry about unpaid bills, their capacity for hard work is so enormous they can hardly help but achieve a great deal, and before very long they find themselves well off and regarded with respect by everyone in the community. If these types could only manage to unwind, be gentle with themselves and enjoy their success, they could be very happy indeed.

Aquarius Ox

The Ox has never been a flashy sign. These types believe actions speak louder than words, and they like to beaver away without drawing attention to themselves. When this trait is coupled with the slightly introverted though idealistic nature of Aquarius, you get a quiet, complex character who prefers to work behind the scenes and turns modest when the limelight is switched on. Never known for his verbal dexterity, the Ox born under Aquarius can suddenly turn into a persuasive orator when a humanitarian cause sparks unexpected passion. These types make loyal, faithful companions to those who take the trouble to understand them and their intelligence and dogged persistence makes them invaluable as researchers, political assistants and private secretaries.

Pisces Ox

Few Oxen can be described as fey, changeable creatures but those that come the closest will be found under the sign of Pisces. Pisces brings an emotional, artistic quality to the steadfast Ox. These types are loving, faithful and true, yet it is often difficult to guess what they are thinking. Of all the Ox family, Pisces Oxen are likely to be the most moody and yet in many ways also the most creative. The Ox input lends strength and stamina to more delicate Pisces constitutions, enabling them to accomplish far more than other Pisces subjects. Just leave them alone until they're ready to face the world.

Tiger

Aries Tiger

Another combination which could be potentially explosive but, in this case, energetic Aries adds force and power to the Tiger's humanitarian instincts while the Tiger's unworldly nature curbs Aries materialistic streak. These types really could change the world for the better if they put their minds to it. They are kind and thoughtful, and while they might be impatient at times, they quickly regret any harsh words spoken in the heat of the moment.

Taurus Tiger

Taurus Tigers are tremendous achievers. The strength of the zodiac bull added to the fire of the Tiger produces a truly formidable individual who can do almost anything to which he sets his mind. These types often end up making a great deal of money. They have to work hard for all their gains, but this doesn't worry them at all. They also take a great deal of pleasure in spending their hard-earned cash. They like to share what they've got, and this gives them such childish joy that no-one begrudges them their good fortune.

Gemini Tiger

The quicksilver mind of Gemini adds zing and extra flexibility to the Tiger's powerful individualism. These Tigers are blessed with minds which overflow with brilliant ideas. They are creative and often artistic too, so they're capable of wonderful achievements. Their only drawback is that they possess almost too much of a good thing. They have so many ideas that they tend to zoom off at a tangent onto a new task before they have completed the one on which they were working.

Cancer Tiger

These Tigers are immensely clever but a little more retiring than the usual bold, brave terror of the jungle. No Tiger is timid, but Cancer has the effect of quietening the more reckless excesses of the Tiger and allowing a little caution to creep into the blend. They still like a challenge but will opt for something a little less physically demanding than other Tigers. These types are more able to fit into society and tolerate authority better than other Tigers, and for this reason they often do well in their careers.

Leo Tiger

What would you get if you crossed a lion with a tiger? A very wild beast indeed. Some sort of striped wonder of the world no doubt! Leo Tigers certainly make their mark. Tigers are big, beautiful, fearless personalities who crave the limelight and love to be noticed. They believe in doing good deeds, but they like to be noticed doing them. These are not the types of which anonymous benefactors are made. When the Leo Tiger raises money for charity, he likes to make sure the world's press are gathered to record the occasion if at all possible. Yet his heart's in the right place. Let these Tigers have their share of praise, and they will work wonders for others.

Virgo Tiger

The Virgo Tiger is quite a different beast. Virgo accentuates the Tiger's already well-developed sense of justice. These types cannot rest until wrongdoers have got their just deserts. They often go into professions involving the law and the police force. They are immensely self-disciplined and have very high standards. Totally trustworthy and effective, they can sometimes be a little difficult to live with. They are not unkind; it's just that they expect everyone else to be as perfect as they are themselves. Yet Virgo adds attention-to-detail to Tiger's passion to change the world, and the combination creates a character who really could make a lasting difference.

Libra Tiger

Laidback Libra brings quite a different quality to the Tiger. Tiger's intensity is softened by pure Libra charm, and the result is a Tiger of unrivalled compassion and magnetism. Libra Tigers often end up in the caring professions where people flock to them with relief. These Tigers want to help, and Libra gives them the ability to understand just what people need and when. You'd never catch a Libra Tiger helping an old lady across the road who didn't wish to go. Libra Tiger would realise at once that the woman was waiting for a bus, would stand with her to keep her company, help her on when the vehicle arrived and make sure the driver put her off at the right stop. No wonder these Tigers are so well-loved wherever they go.

Scorpio Tiger

Crossing a Scorpion with a Tiger is a very tricky proposition. These types mean well, but they are often misunderstood. Scorpio brings a tremendous depth of feeling to the Tiger's reforming instincts, but this sometimes causes them to put tremendous effort into the wrong causes with alarming results. These types can be very quick-tempered, and they may nurse a grudge for a long time. They never forgive disloyalty, and they never forget. It would be a serious mistake to make an enemy of a Scorpio Tiger – but once this individual becomes a friend, they'll be loyal for life.

Sagittarius Tiger

Another charmer, the Sagittarius Tiger is nevertheless likely to hit the road at the slightest opportunity. These types are wanderers, and no matter how much they seem to enjoy company, they enjoy moving on even more. They can't bear working for other people and do far better being self-employed. The travel industry would suit them perfectly. Impossible to cage in or pin down – don't even try – the only way to have a happy relationship with a Sagittarius Tiger is to make them feel free at all times.

Capricorn Tiger

Steady Capricorn lends a prudent touch to the impulsive Tiger, and these types are the Tigers most likely to stop and think before rushing off to save the rain forest. They still enjoy improving the world, but they check travel arrangements, make sure they have got sufficient funds and do a bit of research online first. These are not party animals. While they enjoy company, they prefer serious discussion to frivolous small talk and much as they enjoy travel, they appreciate the comfort of home. These Tigers like to develop their theories from the depths of their favourite armchair beside their own cosy hearth.

Aquarius Tiger

When idealistic Aquarius meets idealistic Tiger, you have to hang onto that long tiger tail to keep these subjects, feet on the ground. These types really do have their heads in the clouds and are totally unpredictable. Once a worthwhile cause presents itself, they will rush off immediately without a thought to the consequences. Convention is of no interest to them. They couldn't care less what other people think. They go through life guided entirely by a strong inner sense of right and wrong. If it's right, they know it without a shadow of a doubt; if it's wrong, they will not do it no matter what anyone says. This attitude can get them into a lot of trouble, but other signs sneakily admire their courage. People may not agree with Aquarius Tiger, but no one can doubt his integrity.

Pisces Tiger

One of Tiger's failings is a tendency to be indecisive without warning, and this trait is heightened in Pisces Tigers. These types are anxious to do the right thing; it's just that sometimes it's very difficult to know what that right thing is. There are so many alternatives. Pisces Tiger is kind and gentle and apt to get sentimental at times. They want to save the world, but they'd like someone alongside to help them – though not too many. Despite their indecision, they usually end up heading in the right direction in the end. Yet, even when they've achieved a great deal, they still agonise over whether they could have done even more.

Rabbit

Aries Rabbit

This is a very dynamic Rabbit. When powerful Aries injects a streak of energy into that cultured Rabbit personality, the result is a wonderfully clever individual who glides effortlessly to success. Although at times Aries Rabbit has an attack of over-cautiousness, these types are usually bolder than the average bunny and achieve much where other Rabbits might run away. Occasionally, these Rabbits will even take a gamble, and this is worthwhile as it usually pays off for them.

Taurus Rabbit

The Taurus Rabbit really does feel his home is his castle. He is not unduly interested in his career, but he is likely to turn his home into an art form. Brilliant entertainers, these types guarantee their lucky guests will enjoy all the creature comforts possible. They often marry later in life than average, but when they do, they work at the relationship. Providing they choose another home bird, they are likely to be very happy.

Gemini Rabbit

All Rabbits are natural diplomats, but the Gemini Rabbit really is the star of them all. So skilled a communicator is this creature, so expert at people management that a career in the diplomatic service, politics, psychology or even advertising is an option. Never lost for words, these types can persuade anyone to do almost anything. As a result, they are usually very successful. Once they harness their enviable skills to a worthwhile career, they can go far.

Cancer Rabbit

Cancer Rabbits are gentle, kindly souls. They like to be surrounded by pleasant company and prefer to have few demands put upon them. They don't really take to business life and find many professions too abrasive. On the other hand, they find working for themselves too stressful a venture to be considered seriously. They are happiest in a peaceful, routine environment where they can make steady progress, but really their hearts are at home. Home is where they express themselves.

Leo Rabbit

Leo Rabbits, on the other hand, are usually very popular with a wide circle of friends. Extrovert Leo gives Rabbit a strong dose of confidence and flair, and when these qualities are added to Rabbit's people skills, a radiant, magnetic individual is born. Leo Rabbits adore parties where they shine. They are always elegant and beautifully turned out and have a knack of putting others at their ease. These Rabbits climb the ladder of success very quickly.

Virgo Rabbit

Virgo Rabbits have a lot on their minds. The natural cautiousness of the Rabbit is heightened by the same quality in Virgo, and these Rabbits tend to be born worriers. They are masters of detail but, unfortunately, this often leads them to make mountains out of molehills. They are very talented creatures but too often fail to make the best use of their gifts because they spend so much time worrying about all the things that could go wrong. If they can learn to relax and take the odd risk now and then, they will go far.

Libra Rabbit

Art-loving Libra blends easily into the cultured sign of the Rabbit. These types love to learn more about beautiful things, and they like to share their knowledge with others. They are so good with people that they can convey information effortlessly and make the dullest subject sound interesting. These types are often gifted teachers and lecturers though they would find difficult inner-city schools too traumatic. Give these types willing and interested pupils, and they blossom.

Scorpio Rabbit

Rabbits tend to be discreet people, and Scorpio Rabbits are the most tight-lipped of the lot. Scorpio Rabbits have a lot of secrets, and they enjoy keeping them. It gives them a wonderful feeling of superiority to think that they know things others don't. They have many secret ambitions too, and they don't like to speak of them in case others are pessimistic and pour scorn on their plans. So, it is the Scorpio Rabbit who is most likely to surprise everyone by suddenly reaching an amazing goal that no-one even knew he was aiming for.

Sagittarius Rabbit

Sporty Sagittarius brings a whole new dimension to the art-loving Rabbit. Rabbits are often indoor creatures, but Sagittarian Rabbits are much more adventurous in the open air than the usual bunny. They are sensuous and fun and attract many friends. They are also versatile and can turn their hands to several different careers if necessary. They like to get out and about more than most Rabbits and they are usually very successful.

Capricorn Rabbit

Capricorn Rabbits are great family folk. They firmly believe the family is the bedrock of life, and they work hard to keep their relations happy and together. The Capricorn Rabbit home is the centre of numerous clan gatherings throughout the year and weddings, birthdays, anniversaries and christenings are very important to them. Capricorn Rabbit will never forget the dates. These types are particularly interested in the past and will enjoy researching a family tree going back generations. If it ever crosses their minds that the rest of the tribe seems to leave all the donkey work to Capricorn Rabbit, he'd never say so. And, in truth, he doesn't really mind. There's nothing he loves more than having his family around him.

Aquarius Rabbit

The Aquarius Rabbit is a contradictory creature being both cautious and curious at the same time. These types crave security and love, and yet they have a great longing to find out more about everything around them. Fascinated by art, science and new inventions they love to potter about in book shops and tinker in the shed at home. Once they get an idea in their head, they can't rest until they have experimented with it, frequently forgetting to eat while they work. They need love and understanding.

Pisces Rabbit

The Pisces Rabbit is another bunny who needs a lot of understanding. Often gifted artistically they can sometimes be stubborn and awkward for no apparent reason. Yet when they are in the right frame of mind, they can charm the birds off the trees. It takes them a long time to make a friend, but when they do, it is a friend for life. The Pisces Rabbit home is full of beautiful things, and these subjects love to invite their most trusted friends to come and enjoy the magic.

Dragon

Aries Dragon

The Dragon is already a powerful sign, but when the lively influence of Aries is added, you have a positively devastating individual. These are the types that others either love or loathe. Strong, confident people can cope happily with the Aries Dragon, but more timid souls are terrified. The Aries Dragon himself is quite unaware of the reaction he causes. He goes busily on his way oblivious of the earthquakes all around him. These types have to guard against arrogance, particularly since they have quite a lot to be arrogant about. They also have a tendency to get bored easily and move on to new projects without completing the old, which is a pity since they can accomplish much if they persevere.

Taurus Dragon

There is something magnificent about the Taurus Dragon. Large, expansive types, they move easily around the social scene spreading bonhomie wherever they go. Not the most sensitive of individuals, they find it difficult to assess the moods of others and assume everyone else feels the same way they do. Should it be brought to their attention that someone is unhappy, however, they will move heaven and earth to cheer them up. These types are reliable and conscientious and always keep their promises.

Gemini Dragon

Dragons may not have the quickest minds in the Chinese zodiac, but Gemini Dragons are speedier than most. They are jovial types with a brilliant sense of humour. In fact, they can cleverly joke others into doing what they want. These types have no need for physical force to get their own way; they use laughter instead. At times, Gemini Dragons can be almost devious, which is unusual for a Dragon but nobody really minds their schemes. They give everyone such a good time on the way it's worth doing what they want for the sheer entertainment.

Cancer Dragon

Cautious Cancer and flamboyant Dragon make a surprisingly good combination. Cancer holds Dragon back where he might go too far, while Dragon endows the Crab with exuberance and style. These types like to help others make the most of themselves, but they are also high achievers in their own right. Without upsetting anyone, Cancer Dragons tend to zoom to the top faster than most.

Leo Dragon

This Dragon is so dazzling you need sunglasses to look at him. The proud, glorious Lion combined with the magnificent Dragon is an extraordinary combination, and it's fortunate it only comes around once every twelve years. Too many of such splendid creatures would be hard to take. Leo Dragons really do have star quality, and they know it. They demand to be the centre of attention and praise is like oxygen to them – they can't live without it. Yet they have generous hearts, and if anyone is in trouble, Leo Dragon will be the first to rush to their assistance.

Virgo Dragon

Unusually for a Dragon, the Virgo variety can get quite aggressive if crossed, but this doesn't often happen as very few people would dare take on such a daunting beast. These types are immensely clever in business. They steadily add acquisition to shrewd acquisition until they end up seriously rich. They are wilier than most Dragons who have a surprisingly naive streak, and they make the most of it. These types just can't help becoming successful in whatever they undertake.

Libra Dragon

Dragons are not usually too bothered about trifles such as fine clothes and wallpaper. In fact, some older, more absent-minded Dragons have been known to go shopping in their slippers having forgotten to take them off. The exception is the Dragon born under the sign of Libra. These types are more down to earth and see the sense in putting on a good show for others. They take the trouble to choose smart clothes and keep them looking that way at all times. They are also more intuitive and are not easily fooled by others.

Scorpio Dragon

Handling money is not a Dragon strong point, but the Scorpio variety has more ability in this direction than most. Scorpio Dragons enjoy amassing cash. Rather like their legendary namesakes who hoard treasure in their lairs, Scorpio Dragons like to build substantial nest-eggs and keep them close at hand where they can admire them regularly. These types can also be a little stingy financially, not out of true meanness but simply because they don't like to see their carefully guarded heap diminish in size. Once they understand the importance of a purchase, however, they can be just as generous as their brothers and sisters.

Sagittarius Dragon

When Sagittarius joins the Dragon, the combination produces a real livewire, a true daredevil. The antics of the Sagittarius Dragon, when young, will give their mothers nightmares and later drive their partners to drink. These types can't resist a challenge, particularly a dangerous one. They will climb mountain peaks, leap off cliffs on a hang-glider and try a spot of bungee-jumping to enliven a dull moment. It's no good expecting these types to sit down with a good book; they just can't keep still. However, surrounded by friends, dashing from one perilous venture to the next, the Sagittarius Dragon is one of the happiest people around.

Capricorn Dragon

The Capricorn Dragon looks back at his Sagittarian brother in horror. He simply can't understand the need for such pranks. Being Dragons, these types are bold, but the influence of Capricorn ensures that they are never foolhardy. They look before they leap and occasionally miss a good deal because they stop to check the fine print. They are not the most intuitive of creatures, but show them a needy soul and they will efficiently do whatever's necessary to help. The Capricorn Dragon is a highly effective creature.

Aquarius Dragon

Happy go lucky types, the Aquarius Dragons are usually surrounded by people. Honest and hardworking, they will put in just as much effort for very little cash as they will for a great deal. If someone asks them to do a job and they agree to do it, they will move heaven and earth to fulfil their obligations even if it is not in their best interests to do so. However, they're not suited to routine, and if a task doesn't interest them, they will avoid it at all costs no matter how well paid it might be. Not particularly interested in money for its own sake, these types are sociable and easy to get along with. They are often highly talented in some way.

Pisces Dragon

Pisces Dragons, on the other hand, are surprisingly good with cash. Despite their often vague, good-humoured exteriors these types have excellent financial brains and seem to know just what to do to increase their savings. They are first in the queue when bargains are to be found, and they seem to sense what the next money-making trend is going to be before anyone else has thought of it. These types often end up quite wealthy and excel, particularly, in artistic fields.

Snake

Aries Snake

Generally speaking, Snakes tend to lack energy, so the influence of dynamic Aries is very welcome indeed. These subjects are highly intelligent, well-motivated and never leave anything unfinished. They are achievers and will not give up until they reach their goal – which they invariably do. Nothing can stand in the way of Aries Snakes, and they reach the top of whatever tree they climb.

Taurus Snake

In contrast, the sensuous Taurus Snake really can't be bothered with all that hard work. Taurus Snakes have great ability, but they will only do as much as is necessary to acquire the lifestyle they desire, and then they like to sit back and enjoy it. Tremendous sun worshippers, the Taurus Snakes would be quite happy to be on a permanent holiday, providing the accommodation was a five-star hotel with a fabulous restaurant.

Gemini Snake

The Gemini Snake can be a slippery customer. A brilliant brain, linked to a shrewd but amusing tongue, these types can run rings around almost everybody. They can scheme and manipulate if it suits them and pull off all sorts of audacious tricks but having achieved much, they tend to get bored and lose interest, giving up on the brink of great things. This often leads to conflict with business associates who cannot understand such contradictory behaviour. Insane they call it. Suicidal. The Gemini Snake just shrugs and moves on.

Cancer Snake

The Snake born under the sign of Cancer is a more conventional creature. These types will at least do all that is required of them and bring their formidable Snake brains to bear on the task in hand. They are gifted researchers, historians and archaeologists – any career which involves deep concentration and patient study. But the Cancer Snake must take care to mix with cheerful people since left to himself he has a tendency for melancholy. Warmth, laughter, and plenty of rest transforms the Cancer Snake and allows those unique talents to blossom.

Leo Snake

The Leo Snake is a very seductive creature. Beautifully dressed, sparklingly magnetic, few people can take their eyes off these types, and they know it. All Snakes are sensuous, but the Snake born under the sign of Leo is probably the most sensuous of the lot. Never short of admirers, these types are not eager to settle down. Why should they when they're having such a good time? Late in life, the Leo Snake may consent to get married if their partner can offer them a good enough life. If not, these types are quite content to go it alone – probably because they are never truly on their own. They collect willing followers right into old age.

Virgo Snake

The Virgo Snake is another fascinating combination. Highly intuitive and wildly passionate, the Virgo Snake is all elegant understatement on the outside and erotic abandon on the inside. The opposite sex is mesmerised by this intriguing contradiction and just can't stay away. Virgo Snakes can achieve success in their careers if they put their minds to it, but often they are having too much fun flirting and flitting from one lover to the next. Faithfulness is not their strong point, but they are so sexy they get away with murder.

Libra Snake

When you see a top model slinking sinuously down the catwalk, she could very well be a Libra Snake. Snakes born under this sign are the most elegant and stylish of the lot. They may not be conventionally good looking, but they will turn heads wherever they go. These types really understand clothes and could make a plastic bin-liner look glamorous just by putting it on. Somehow, they have the knack of stepping off a transatlantic flight without a crease and driving an open-topped sports car without ruffling their hair. No-one knows quite how they achieve these feats, and Libra Snake isn't telling.

Scorpio Snake

The Snake born under Scorpio is destined to have a complicated life. These types enjoy plots and intrigues, particularly of a romantic nature and spend endless hours devising schemes and planning subterfuge. That ingenious Snake brain is capable of brewing up the most elaborate scams, and there's nothing Scorpio Snake loves more than watching all the parts fall into place. But schemes have a knack of going wrong, and schemers have to change their plans and change them again to cope with each new contingency as it arises. If he's not careful, the Scorpio Snake can become hopelessly embroiled in his own plot.

Sagittarius Snake

Traditionally other signs are wary of the Snake and tend to hold back a little from them without knowing why. When the Snake is born under Sagittarius, however, the subject seems more approachable than most. Sagittarian Snakes sooner or later become recognised for their wisdom and down to earth good sense and people flock to them for advice. Without ever intending to, the Sagittarius Snake could end up as something of a guru attracting eager acolytes desperate to learn more.

Capricorn Snake

The Snake born under Capricorn is more ambitious than the average serpent. These types will reach for the stars and grasp them. Obstacles just melt away when faced with the dual-beam of Capricorn Snake intelligence and quiet persistence. These Snakes are good providers and more dependable than most Snakes. They often end up surrounded by all the trappings of success, but they accomplish this so quietly, no one can quite work out how they managed it.

Aquarius Snake

Another highly intuitive Snake. Independent but people-loving Aquarius endows the serpent with greater social skills than usual. These types attract many friends, and they have the ability to understand just how others are feeling without them having to say a word. These Snakes have particularly enquiring minds, and they can't pass a museum or book shop without going in to browse. Born researchers, they love to dig and delve into whatever subject has taken their fancy, no matter how obscure. Quite often, they discover something valuable by accident.

Pisces Snake

Pisces Snakes tend to live on their nerves even more than most. These types are friendly up to a point, but they hate disagreements and problems and withdraw when things look unpleasant. They are sexy and sensuous and would much prefer a quiet evening with just one special person than a wild party. In the privacy of their bedroom, anything goes, and Pisces Snakes reveal the naughty side of their characters. No one would guess from the understated elegance of their exteriors what an erotic creature the Pisces Snake really is.

CHAPTER 17: CREATE A WONDERFUL YEAR

By now, you should have a pretty good idea of the main zodiac influences on your lifestyle and personality, according to Chinese astrology. But how is 2026 going to shape up for you in general? Well, that largely depends on how cleverly you play your hand.

Horse years are traditionally regarded as fortunate, action-packed and fast-moving. Suddenly, a desire for independence and freedom seizes the world, and even previously stoic types are likely to be swept along by the mood. Restless undercurrents gradually build to create the lasting changes people realise they've been wanting to make for years.

So far, so fortunate, but as we're always being told, it's dangerous to play with fire. While embracing beneficial changes, it's sensible to keep a little caution in reserve. The Horse can be a shade crazy at times, and fire can easily rage out of control. While keeping one foot firmly on the gas, it's prudent to have the other hovering near the brake pedal. Be prepared to make an emergency stop if necessary.

The key point is that – according to Chinese astrology – everything should be in balance. So, after the complicated, convoluted, sometimes treacherous, sometimes secretive machinations of the Snake year, the world is ready for the antidote.

In 2026, the emphasis will be on transparency, straightforward behaviour, a simple 'it-does what-it-says-on-the-tin' attitude and a 'just-get-on-with-it' approach. Business leaders and politicians who try to obfuscate with weasel words will spark anger rather than support. Impatience rules. All talk and no action types will get nowhere, while those who move quickly and decisively are likely to enjoy rewards even if they don't succeed one hundred percent. The Horse appreciates genuine effort if it's sincere.

Some signs will find these conditions more comfortable than others. Zodiac creatures that prefer to take their time, examine the small print and weigh up a number of options before committing themselves could find the pace nerve-racking. While the leap straight in, make-it-up-as-you-go-along, adrenaline junkies will thrive – as long as they manage not to crash and burn along the way, that is. Yet, whichever group you belong to, as long as you're prepared – and you know what you might be up against – you can develop a strategy to ride those waves like a world-class surfer.

Sit back and rely on good fortune alone, because it's a terrific year for your sign, and you could snatch failure from the jaws of success.

Navigate any stormy seas with skill and foresight if it's not such a sunny year for your sign, and you'll sail on to fulfil your dreams.

This is always true in any year, but doubly so when the dynamic Horse is in charge. Be quick, decisive, and courageous, yet prepared to hit pause should danger threaten, and the Horse will smile on you.

So, no matter what zodiac sign you were born under, the luck of the Horse will help you... if you help yourself.

The future is not set in stone.

Chinese astrology is used very much like a weather forecast. You check out the likely conditions you'll encounter on your journey through the year, and plan your route and equipment accordingly. Some signs might need a parasol, sunscreen, and sandals; others might require stout walking boots and rain gear.

Yet, properly prepared, both will end up in a good place at the end of the trip.

Finally, it's said that if you feel another sign has a much better outlook than you this year, you can carry a small symbol of that animal with you (in the form of a piece of jewellery, perhaps, or a tiny charm in your pocket or bag) and their good luck will rub off on you. Does it work? For some, maybe, but there's certainly no harm in trying.

Other Books from the Publisher

Linda Dearsley – *the author of this book* – was Doris Stokes' ghost.

Well, more accurately, she was the ghost-writer for Doris Stokes and worked with her for 10 years to produce 7 books, detailing the great lady's life.

In Voices Everywhere, Linda shines a light on her time working with Doris, right from the very early days when Doris was doing private readings in her Fulham flat, to filling the London Palladium and Barbican night after night, to subsequent fame outside the UK. Throughout all this, Doris Stokes never became anyone other than who she was: a kind, generous, and down-to-earth woman with an extraordinary gift, and a fondness for a nice cup of tea. January 6th, 2020, would have been Doris' 100th birthday.

Following Doris' death, Linda chronicles how cynics tried to torpedo the Stokes legacy with accusations of cheating and dishonesty, but how those closest to Doris never believed she was anything other than genuine.

In turn, as the months and years rolled by, more and more intriguing people crossed Linda's path, each with their own unexplainable power, and Doris never seemed far away. From the palmist who saw pictures in people's hands, to the couple whose marriage was predicted by Doris, and the woman who believes she captures departed spirits on camera – the mysterious world of the paranormal, and Doris Stokes' place within it, continues to unfold.

Karina Collins is an acclaimed Tarot reader who has helped people, from all walks of life, to better understand their lives' journeys.

Now, she is on a mission to help you take control of your life – through the power of Tarot – to better explore and understand your purpose and destiny.

Do you have questions about now and your future? Perhaps about making more money, or whether love is on the horizon, or whether you will become happier? Do you want to steer your life in a direction that brings success, pleasure, and fulfilment? Well, Tarot is a means to help you do exactly that! Used for centuries, it provides a powerful tool for unlocking knowledge, divining the future, and delivering shortcuts to the lives we desire.

In this full-colour top-rated book, Karina provides explanations and insights into the full 78-card Tarot deck, how to phrase questions most effectively, real-world sample readings, why seemingly scary cards represent opportunities for growth and triumph, and more.

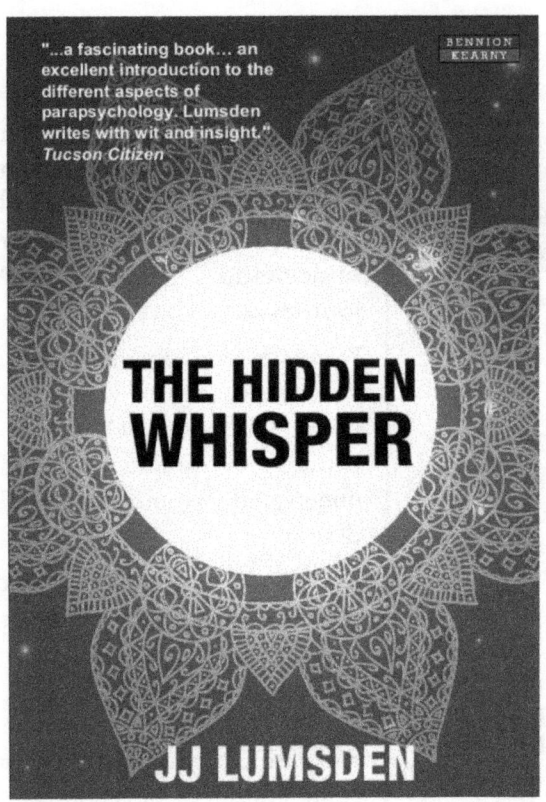

A paranormal puzzle smoulders in the desert heat of southern Arizona. At the home of Jack and Chloe Monroe, a written message "Leave Now" appears then disappears, a candle in an empty room mysteriously lights itself, and – most enigmatically – an unidentifiable ethereal whisper begins to permeate the house. What was once simply strange now feels sinister. What once seemed a curiosity now seems terrifying.

Dr. Luke Jackson, a British Parapsychologist visiting family nearby, is asked to investigate and quickly finds himself drawn deeper into the series of unexplained events. Time is against him. He has just one week to understand and resolve the poltergeist case before he must depart Arizona.

The Hidden Whisper is the acclaimed paranormal thriller, written by real-life parapsychologist Dr. JJ Lumsden, which offers a rare opportunity to enter the intriguing world of parapsychology through the eyes of Luke Jackson. The fictional narrative is combined with extensive endnotes and references that cover Extra Sensory Perception, Psychokinesis, Haunts, Poltergeists, Out of Body Experiences, and more. If you thought parapsychology was like Ghostbusters – think again…

"This book works on many levels, an excellent introduction to the concepts current in the field of parapsychology… at best you may learn something new, and at worst you'll have read a witty and well-written paranormal detective story" Parascience.

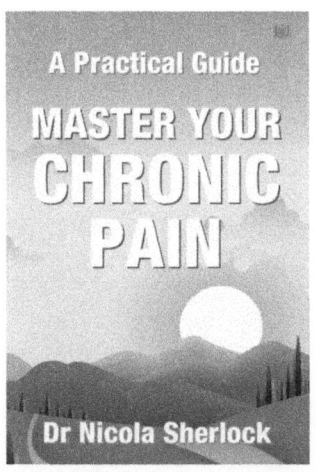
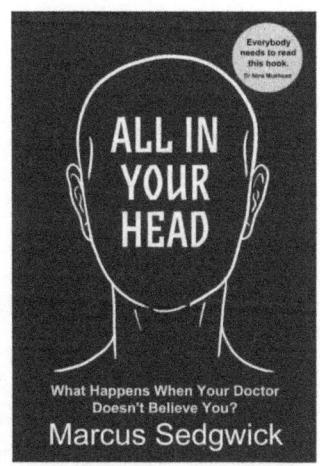

www.ingramcontent.com/pod-product-compliance
Lightning Source LLC
Chambersburg PA
CBHW032225080426
42735CB00008B/711